Minute Meditations for Men

BOB BARNES

HARVEST HOUSE PUBLISHERS
Eugene, Oregon 97402

MINUTE MEDITATIONS FOR MEN
Copyright © 1998 by Bob Barnes
Published by Harvest House Publishers
Eugene, Oregon 97402

Library of Congress Cataloging-in-Publication Data

Barnes, Bob, 1933–
    Minute meditations for men / Bob Barnes
        p. cm.
    ISBN 1-56507-863-2
    1. Men—Prayer-books and devotions—English. 2. Devotional calendars. I. Title.
BV4843.B375   1998
242'.642—dc21   97-44732
                                                                                        CIP

This book is dedicated to my son, Brad.

It has been such a delight to see God work in Brad's life from the time he was a small boy to now as a grown man. My son travels extensively, and the short meditations in this book will help him get started in the morning or wind down after a busy day. These thoughts will encourage him as a father and husband through the many facets of life. Brad will be the conduit of my thoughts to the next generation.

Love,
Dad

A Note from the Author

As men uniquely created by God, we know we should give God, wives, and children high priority, but we often feel guilty because there's always something that demands that time and space.

Oh, I try so hard to find time, but by the end of another hectic day, I realize that I haven't given adequate time to all those who really love me.

After writing my book, *Fifteen Minutes Alone with God for Men*, I had a lot of men tell me that the format was really an improvement over any other book on the market, but they needed something even shorter. Thus came *Minute Meditations for Men*. A combination of new material and excerpts from *15 Minutes*, these short devotions are designed to be read while shaving, riding the subway, riding in the elevator in the office building, or having a short midmorning break. It is so very important that we establish a daily routine where we pause and let God speak to us through His Word.

As in my past devotionals, I have placed three boxes in the top portion of each devotion so you can check off each devotion after you've read it. This way you can keep track of what you've read. This system also gives you the freedom to choose devotions that fit your need for that day.

Each brief devotion carries a nugget of truth. You may say your own prayer, or you can use mine to close your study.

May God richly bless your life as you enter into a daily walk with Him.

Bob Barnes

To Give and to Serve

*For even the Son of Man came not to be minis-
tered unto, but to minister, and to give his life a
ransom for many.*

—Mark 10:45 KJV

————◇————

O ne of the main purposes of Christian life is to serve. The secular world usually wants to be served, but just as Jesus came to serve so are we to minister to those around us. The story is told of the man who rushed to the church door and asked if the service was over. The wise usher replied, "The worship is over, but the service is only beginning." The service we render to others is really the rent we pay for our rooms on this earth. It is obvious that man is a traveler, and that the purpose of this world is not "to have and to hold" but "to give and to serve." There can be no other meaning.

Today's Action

- ◆ Identify one person whom you can serve today. Then go out and do it.

Prayer

Father God, place a desire in my heart to be a servant unto people. Give me that opportunity today. Amen.

Godly Honor

*Jesus said to them, "You do not know what you
are asking for. Are you able to drink the cup that
I drink. . .?"*

—Mark 10:38

————◇————

Many times we ask for things not realizing the price to be
paid if we get our requests. James and John had asked
Jesus if they could sit at His right and left, not realizing the
cost of that request. They wanted the honor of sitting so close
to Jesus, but they had no idea that a cross had to be borne
along with that honor.

Many times we pray to be the best husband, the best work-
er, the best baseball player, the best salesman, or the best father
without taking the time to figure out what cost our request
will make on our lives.

Great requests or supplications with shallow motives can
turn out to be very overwhelming when answered by God.
Also, great requests or supplications with stately motives for
God's grace may often be granted—but not in the way we
might expect.

Godly honor is not lightly won; we must be ready to pay
the price in time, trials, sacrifice, love, and money.

Today's Action

- ◆ Make sure you realize what the costs might be *before* you
  ask God for something.

Prayer

*Father God, thanks for making me aware of the cost of serving
others. Help me take time today to count the cost for being one of
Your disciples—then give You praise for allowing me to serve You.
Amen.*

A Dependable Man

I will give you a new heart.

—Ezekiel 36:26

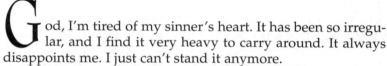

God, I'm tired of my sinner's heart. It has been so irregular, and I find it very heavy to carry around. It always disappoints me. I just can't stand it anymore.

I plead for a new heart that considers and loves other people more than myself. I want it to blend in with my Christian friends, so that the tangles that now exist will be gone. Like the psalmist, I ask, "Please give me a steadfast spirit that will always be consistent and dependable. I'm tired of being a flake to others. I want to be a man of dependability—so people will believe what I say."

My desire is to please You, but with my present heart it is most difficult. I need a new beginning. You are the Alpha and the Omega. Help me start anew.

Today's Action

◆ Reach out to God today. Ask for a new heart that truly seeks His will.

Prayer

O my Lord, baptize me in the living water that I may be cleansed of all that separates me from You and Your creation. O Father, "wash me, and I shall be whiter than snow." Amen.

Always or Usually?

□
□
□

> *[Love] always protects, always trusts, always hopes, always perseveres.*
>
> **—1 Corinthians 13:7** NIV

—————◇—————

I t's very hard for us mere mortals to adequately understand the word, *always*. In today's culture we don't adequately understand this kind of commitment. When we say *always*, don't we usually mean sometimes . . . or most of the time? But *always* really means eternal and everlasting. Can anyone commit to always?

When the Scripture says always, it means always. Never changing, dependable until death. I am challenged when Paul writes that love:

- ◆ always protects
- ◆ always trusts
- ◆ always hopes
- ◆ always perseveres

I so want my wife and children to honor me with that kind of love. I want to be a man who is known for his word: "When Dad says something, you can take it to the bank." I often advise, "Just do what you say you are going to do."

As we become older and look back over life's journey, may we know that love and what it encompasses is indeed the true victory of life.

Today's Action

- ◆ Express to your wife and family that with God's help you will *always* love them.

Prayer

Father God, give me the strength and perseverance to truthfully say without hesitation that I will always love my wife and children. Amen.

We Are the Prodigals

While he was still a long way off, his father saw
him and was filled with compassion for him; he
ran to his son, threw his arms around him and
kissed him.

—Luke 15:20 NIV

————◇————

This section from the prodigal son episode is one of the most moving sections in the whole Bible. I can picture the accelerated heartbeat as the father saw his wayward son approaching home after squandering his inheritance money and having to slop pigs to survive. This story reflects our heavenly Father—who runs to us when we are desperate, at rope's end, after having experienced the pitfalls of life, in our pursuit of searching for the true meaning of life. In our search we may not have reached bottom like this son did, but all of us try to find purpose in our own way.

The prodigal tells his father that he is not worthy to be taken back as a son, but that doesn't prevent the father from loving him and forgiving him and bringing out the very best upon his return. This is the way our heavenly Father treats us.

Today's Action
- ◆ Forgive someone for something you considered unforgivable.

Prayer
Father God, thank You for forgiving me while I was in sin.
Amen.

I love you today, where you are and as you are. You do not have to be anything but what you are for me to love you. I love you now; not sometime when you are worthy, but today when you may need love most.

I will not withhold my love or withdraw it. There are no strings on my love, no price. I will not force it upon you when you are not ready. It is just there, freely offered with both hands.

Take what you want today. The more you take, the more there is. It is good if you can return love; but if you cannot today, that is all right too. Love is its own joy. Bless me by letting me love you today.

—*Author unknown*

Rules for Living

Love the Lord your God with all your heart and
with all your soul and with all your mind and
with all your strength. . . .

—Mark 12:30,31 NIV

❏
❏
❏

———◇———

The '90s is a generation of no rules: "Let me do my own thing." "I know what's best for me." "Don't tell me what to do." Today's rule is given as a rule for life. It certainly gives you the boundaries in which to live.

One noted Christian stated, "The rule that governs my life is this: Anything that dims my vision of Christ, or takes away my taste for Bible study, or cramps my prayer life, or makes Christian work difficult, is wrong for me, and I must, as a Christian, turn away from it."

Search your lifestyle today to evaluate how you are doing in your choices of late. Are they drawing you closer or sending you farther away from our Lord? Do you still have the same hunger for God's Word as you used to? Do you still have quiet times with Him? Are your prayers as fervent as before? Do you still enjoy being together with other believers? If not, guess who has moved away?

Today's Action

♦ Evaluate your choices today to see if they will glorify the Lord, Jesus Christ.

Prayer

Father God, let me be honest in my self-appraisal. I don't want to be phony. Amen.

Released from Darkness

He has sent me to bind up the brokenhearted, to proclaim freedom for the captives and release from darkness for the prisoners.

—Isaiah 61:1 NIV

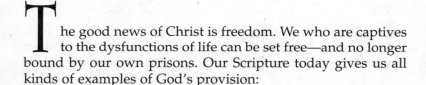

The good news of Christ is freedom. We who are captives to the dysfunctions of life can be set free—and no longer bound by our own prisons. Our Scripture today gives us all kinds of examples of God's provision:

- to bind up the brokenhearted
- to proclaim freedom for the captives
- to release prisoners from the darkness
- to comfort all who mourn
- to bestow a crown of beauty instead of ashes
- to give the oil of gladness instead of mourning
- to give a garment of praise instead of a spirit of despair
- to be called oaks of righteousness, a planting of the Lord

Why? For the display of his splendor. We no longer need to look at the dark side of life. W.R. Alger says, "After every storm the sun will smile; for every problem there is a solution, and the soul's indefensible duty is to be of good cheer." Our glass can be half full when others see it as half empty.

Today's Action
- Take a negative and make it into a positive.

Prayer
Father God, may those around me see me as an oak of righteousness. Let all that happens to me be a display of Your splendor. Amen.

Secret to Abundance

Whoever sows generously will also reap generously...for God loves a cheerful giver.

—2 Corinthians 9:6,7 NIV

❏
❏
❏

———◇———

This is not only a godly principle of life, but it is applicable to the believer as well as the unbeliever. Some of my most generous friends are nonbelievers. They somehow have caught the secret to abundance in life. However, as Christians we have an extra blessing in that God loves a cheerful giver.

Martin Luther said it very well when he stated, "I have held many things in my hands, and I have lost them all; but whatever I have placed in God's hands, that I still possess."

We have a saying around our home, "You can't out-give God." That has been so true by experience. Whenever we give, we seem to reap abundantly from God's riches. As a young man I didn't trust others with my money, time, talent, and possessions—until one day I realized it was all God's in the first place. When I started to trust God with all of these, I found out that He took better care of them than I did.

Today's Action

- ◆ Give something away today with no expectation of return.

Prayer

Father God, help me learn to give generously to those who are in need. I want to be known as a cheerful giver. Amen.

Changing the Negatives

I can do everything through him who gives me
strength.

—Philippians 4:13

———◇———

John Oxenham said it very well in his poem, "The Way":

> To every man there openeth A Way, and Ways and a
> Way. And the High Soul climbs the High Way, and
> the Low Soul gropes the Low, and in between, on
> the misty flats, the rest drift to and fro. But to every
> man there openeth a High Way, and a Low Way.
> And every man decideth the way his soul shall go.

Yes, today we must decide which way we must go—the high way, the middle way, or the low way. Life is full of men who are impaired by poor physical conditions—deaf, blind, crippled, or speech impediments—yet they choose the high way. Because they choose to be victorious, they are written up in the annals of sports, politics, music, art, and drama as contributing greatly to their fields of endeavor. You may be one of those people who have to choose to accept that you can do all things through God who gives you strength.

Today's Action

- ◆ Choose one of your negative attributes and turn it into a positive.

Prayer

Father God, thank You for showing me that life is made up of choices. Today I claim the high way. Amen.

A Hedge of Protection

Do not withhold your mercy from me, O LORD;
may your love and your truth always protect
me.

—Psalm 40:11

———◇———

Our life journey takes us over many roads. Some are paved and don't have chuck holes, others are paved but have lots of holes. Sometimes we travel over dirt roads that are dusty, and some roads even have been muddied by rain.

As you journey each day, ask God to grant you His mercy for the day and to protect you with His love and truth. We have no idea what lies before us, so we need a hedge of protection as we leave home.

Trust God today for your care and share with Him your earthly and human concerns. He cares for you.

Today's Action
◆ Ask God to protect you today from _____.

Prayer
Father God, I claim the promise that You love me and care for me. Do not withhold Your mercy from me this day. Amen.

There are three kinds of givers: the flint, the sponge, and the honeycomb. To get anything out of a flint you must hammer it, and then you get only chips and sparks. To get water out of a sponge you must squeeze it, and the more you squeeze, the more you will get. But the honeycomb just overflows with its own sweetness.

—*The London Christian*

Refreshed by God

*[Elijah] prayed that he might die. Then he lay
down under the tree and fell asleep. All at once an
angel touched him and said, "Get up and eat." He
looked around, and there by his head was a cake of
bread baked over hot coals, and a jar of water.*

—1 Kings 19:4-6 NIV

———◇———

O ften we ask, "Is God really interested in my physical
welfare? Does He care if I eat or sleep?" Yes, God does
care for our personal needs on a daily basis. Much of the
Gospels deal with eating and sleeping. In many situations of
everyday life, Jesus had the same basic needs that we do. After
a hard day's work or journey, He became hungry, thirsty, and
sleepy. We serve a God who, through Jesus, experienced the
same daily requirements that we have.

We must learn to trust Jesus with *all* of our needs. We don't
have to doubt or wonder if He takes care of us in the little
events in life. Scripture shows us very clearly that He cares,
and He will provide for the smallest of needs. What are some
of your smallest needs? Trust Him today for providing for
those concerns.

Today's Action

◆ Trust God today for one of your concerns. Mention it to
Him in prayer.

Prayer

*Father God, thank You for being interested in my needs—I
appreciate Your concern. Amen.*

Praying with Confidence

In the morning, O LORD, you hear my voice; in the morning I lay my requests before you and wait in expectation.

—Psalm 5:3 NIV

———◇———

I often have men ask me, "When should I pray?" The psalmist suggests we pray in the morning. Let God hear your voice and request at the beginning of the day. I certainly don't pray only in the morning. I find myself offering utterances throughout my day and even into the darkest hours. I begin the day with thanksgiving, and I close the day with thanksgiving. Notice also the psalm writer says that he waits in expectation. Expectation for what? Answers to his requests in his morning prayers. Do you pray with the confidence that God hears your voice as you utter your requests? Do you expect God to answer them by nightfall?

> Pray till prayer makes you forget your own wish,
> and leave it or merge it in God's will.

—Fredrick W. Robertson

Today's Action

◆ Pray with expectation.

Prayer

Father God, I don't want selfish requests to come from my lips. May my prayers merge into Your will. Amen.

Strong, Gentle Hands

"He showed them His hands."

—Luke 24:40

❏
❏
❏

————◇————

Do you take your hands for granted? Are your fingers and thumbs just ten appendages that happen to be there? We don't seem to really appreciate what God has given us. We do so much with our hands; even the slightest injury makes us aware of the importance of a finger, thumb, or palm. We can't lift, tie, open, squeeze, or function normally if we can't manipulate our hands as God created them to be.

I know that Jesus' hands were human. Because of His carpentry trade and His journeying in the hot Mediterranean climate of the Middle East, they were strong and rough. Even though they were not soft and manicured, His hands blessed the little ones; His hands touched the sick and made them well in mind, spirit, and body. In John 10:28 He gives us a picture of His saving hands: "I give them eternal life, and they shall never perish, no one can snatch them out of my hands" (NIV).

Jesus took from the cross wounded hands that paid the price for our sins. As we look at our hands today, may we remember the price Jesus paid with His hands.

Today's Action
◆ Look at your hands and thank God for them.
Prayer
Father God, I thank You for my hands. May I use them to Your glory. Amen.

An Inheritance Challenge

A good man leaves an inheritance for his children's children.

—Proverbs 13:22 NIV

Not too many years ago I was challenged to have a trust and a will drawn up by an attorney who specializes in these areas. I knew that because of the way our taxes are structured, if something would happen to Emilie and me, our estate would be locked up in a mountain of laws and regulations.

As we decided how our estate would be divided, this particular verse of Scripture challenged us to leave part of our worldly possessions to our five grandchildren. Not only were they listed as beneficiaries, but we set up an account with our stockbroker and have contributed monies on a timely basis for their birthdays and Christmas. In the process, they are learning about mutual funds and the stock market. What a delight to see them take an interest in financial matters.

Today's Action

- ◆ Set up a provision to include your grandchildren in your inheritance.

Prayer

Father God, thank You for giving me an abundance so I can share with others. Amen.

But As for Me...

> *But if serving the Lord seems undesirable to you, then choose for yourselves this day whom you will serve, whether the gods your forefathers served beyond the River, or the gods of the Amorites, in whose land you are living. But as for me and my household, we will serve the Lord.*
>
> **—Joshua 24:15** NIV

❏
❏
❏

J oshua was a wise man because in his latter days of life he knew that his countrymen would follow some type of god. He made a very strong public declaration that he and his family were going to serve the Lord.

Dads, we need to be so bold with our family. How many wives and children are waiting patiently for husbands and dads to step forward and make the same declaration? In the past 20 years more and more men have been giving their wives that responsibility. However, the Scripture is very clear—that responsibility belongs to us as husbands and fathers.

Men, step forward and declare to all those within listening ears that you are going to take the initiative and declare which God your family will serve.

Today's Action
- ◆ Today, declare that you and your household will serve the Lord.

Prayer
Father God, thank You for this challenge. Give me a brave heart in making this proclamation. Amen.

A man is a success who has lived well,
laughed often and loved much; who has
gained the respect of intelligent men
and the love of children; who has filled
his niche and accomplished his task;
who leaves the world better than he
found it, whether by an improved poppy,
a perfect poem or a rescued soul; who
never lacked appreciation of earth's
beauty or failed to express it; who
looked for the best in others and gave
the best he had.

—*Robert Louis Stevenson*

Raising Healthy Children

By wisdom a house is built, and through understanding it is established; through knowledge its rooms are filled with rare and beautiful treasures.

—Proverbs 24:3,4 NIV

So many couples ask Emilie and me how to raise a healthy family. We always come back to the three basic principles of this passage. We raise our family with:

- wisdom
- understanding
- knowledge

then our rooms are filled with rare and beautiful treasures— children who are obedient, polite, considerate, and honor God.

When we are out in public and observe a healthy, functioning family, we know that they directly or indirectly have been observing these three important guidelines. How do we know that? Because we can see the rewards or blessings of that training. The parents have rare and beautiful treasures. Is it easy to be so blessed? No. It takes a lot of work and stick-to-it discipline to have these treasures. You have to believe in the end results. Emilie and I always go up to the parents of well-mannered kids and compliment them on their efforts. When you see something good, shout it from the housetops.

Today's Action

- Declare today that you are going to raise your children with wisdom, understanding, and knowledge.

Prayer

Father God, I want my rooms to be filled with rare and beautiful treasures. Amen.

Impressed on Our Hearts

Love the Lord your God with all your heart and with all your soul and with all your strength ... Impress [these] on your children. Talk about them when you sit at home and when you walk along the road, when you lie down and when you get up.

—Deuteronomy 6:5-7

————◇————

I n this passage we are encouraged to love the Lord our God with all our hearts and with all our souls and with all our strength. The writer impresses readers to have this command-ment upon their hearts and to teach them to their children by talking to them at home, when taking a walk along the road, when going to bed and when getting up.

Wow, it sounds like we need to be aware of life and be ready to make spiritual applications at all times! Any time and anywhere we can teach godly principles. Use *every* event to talk about the good and bad of life. Help your children develop their own theological grids for life so they can make indepen-dent conclusions on what's right and what's wrong based on the Bible.

Today's Action

- ◆ Choose a current event that has spiritual implications, and teach your children to make sound, God-pleasing conclusions on what's good and what is bad.

Prayer

Father God, help me see spiritual truths I can share in all of life's events. Amen.

Making Godly Decisions

*Seek first his kingdom and his righteousness,
and all these things will be given to you as well.*

—Matthew 6:33

———◇———

I n the "Sermon on the Mount" (Matthew 5–7), Jesus addresses questions regarding concerns about earthly needs such as clothing, food, and what to drink. Jesus replies that pagans run after all these things, but believers depend on the heavenly Father, for their needs. "Therefore do not worry about tomorrow, for tomorrow will worry about itself. Each day has enough trouble of its own," Jesus said. Matthew 6:33 has become our family's theme verse. When in doubt about making a vital decision of life we ask ourselves, "Are we attempting to seek first the kingdom of God, or are we after our own desires?" It's amazing how clear the decision becomes when we ask this basic question. Afterward, within a day or two, it becomes quite clear that we had made the right decision a few days earlier. We find that our children love to have a "family" verse. Matthew 6:33 also helps them when they need to make their own independent decisions.

Today's Action

◆ Choose a family theme verse for your family. Remember, it can always be changed at a later date.

Prayer

Father God, thank You for giving us inspired Scripture that helps us make decisions for life. Amen.

Submission?

Submit to one another out of reverence for Christ.

—Ephesians 5:21

Submission is a very difficult word in today's political climate. No one wants to submit. We all think we know best. Everyone wants to be the quarterback, the captain of the team, the CEO of the firm, the umpire, the boss. It is a very humbling experience to submit. However, throughout Scripture there are numerous places where the term *submit* is used. Even Jesus had to submit to His heavenly Father at the cross! He prayed for "this cup" to pass so He wouldn't have to go to His death. He obeyed God and died for our sins. If He did that for us, we surely can learn to submit one to another out of reverence for Him.

This verse is Emilie's and my favorite marriage verse. Each morning as we wake, we ask ourselves: "How can we submit to each other today?" I help Emilie with laundry, dishes, vacuuming, picking flowers for the table. She helps me by dropping something off at the cleaners, running an errand, or watching one of my favorite sporting events on television.

Today's Action

- ◆ Choose one thing you can do to show submission to your wife.

Prayer

Father God, work on me so I have a more submissive heart. Show me the way. Amen.

Made for the Lord

For he himself is our peace.

—Ephesians 2:14

❑
❑
❑

———◇———

S aint Augustine said, "Lord, thou madest us for thyself, and we can find no rest till we find rest in thee." I just love to come home; our home is so very peaceful. After a hectic day out on the freeway, listening to the loud noises of the world, my heart longs for the comforts of home. I realize that peace doesn't just happen in one's life. I observe friends trying to find peace through their jobs, the toys they buy, the vacations they take, the clothes they wear, and the music they hear. Many of them are looking in all the wrong places. They soon find out that peace is not in these things. Only when they come to realize they were made for the Lord will they find tranquility. There will be no rest or peace for us until we find our Lord.

People often ask, "What is the purpose of life?" Ephesians 2:14 and the quote from Saint Augustine lets us in on the answer. It is to find peace with our Lord. The peacefulness of the Barnes' home is based on the occupants of our home and the fact that all of us have come to know our Lord Jesus Christ.

Today's Action

♦ Be assured that you know Jesus as your Lord. If you haven't or you're not sure, search out a friend who can share what it means to know Jesus or call a local, Bible-based church.

Prayer

Father God, thank You for giving me Your peace. Amen.

Men and women who live together
through long years get to know one
another's failings; but they also come to
know what is worthy of respect and
admiration in those they live with and in
themselves. If at the end one can say,
"This man used to the limit the powers
that God granted him; he was worthy of
love and respect and of the sacrifices
many people made in order that he
might achieve what he deemed to be his
task," then that life has been lived well
and there are no regrets.

—*Eleanor Roosevelt*

The More We Listen ...

*When there are many words, transgression is
unavoidable, but he who restrains his lips is
wise.*

—Proverbs 10:19

❏
❏
❏

————◇————

E leanor Roosevelt, in one of her many speeches stated, "A
mature person is one who does not think only in
absolutes, who is able to be objective even when deeply stirred
emotionally, who has learned that there is both good and bad
in all people and in all things, and who walks humbly and
deals charitably with the circumstances of life. Knowing that
in this world no one is all knowing and therefore all of us need
both love and charity."

Our Scripture verse talks to us about being more of a listener than a talker. Too many words can lead to putting one's
foot in one's mouth. The more we speak, the greater the
chance of being offensive. The wise person will restrain his
speech. God gave us one tongue to speak and two ears to
hear—I guess He wanted us to hear twice as much as we
speak. Listening seldom gets us into trouble, but our mouths
certainly cause transgressions.

Today's Action

◆ Today we are going to concentrate on listening, not
speaking.

Prayer

*Father God, thank You for giving me two good ears to hear. I
want to become a better listener. Amen.*

Singing His Song

*Behold, God is my salvation, I will trust and not
be afraid; for the LORD GOD is my strength and
song.*

—**Isaiah 12:2**

———————◇———————

Billy Graham once stated, "Being a Christian is more than just an instantaneous conversion—it is a daily process whereby you grow to be more and more like Christ." Many men want to know God as a fire insurance policy, but they aren't willing to make Him their Lord. When Jesus becomes our salvation, we receive His courage, strength, and song. It all doesn't happen overnight; it is a lifelong process to become more and more like Christ.

There is a plaque on a cathedral which reads:

Go on your way to peace.
Be of good courage.
Hold fast that which is good.
Render to no man evil for evil.
Strengthen the faint-hearted.
Support the weak.
Help and cheer the sick.
Honor all men.
Love and serve the Lord.
May the blessing of God be upon you and remain
with you forever.

Today's Action

- ◆ Grow to be more and more like Jesus. Trust Him for your courage, strength, and song.

Prayer

Father God, I don't want to be just a Sunday Christian. I want You to give me a new song daily. Thank You for the strength You give me. Amen.

Overcoming Discouragement

*Where can we go? Our brothers have made us
lose heart. They say, "The people are stronger
and taller than we are; the cities are large, with
walls up to the sky."*

—Deuteronomy 1:28

———————◇———————

ven in Moses' time there were negative voices. How
often have you been told that you aren't good enough?
You're too short, your hair is too thin, your lips are too thin,
your voice is too soft, you can't carry a tune, your nose has a
bump on it.

What a misfortune that our friends, teachers, and parents
sometimes put stumbling blocks in our way by discouraging
us with words of fear, guilt, hate, and inferiority. We must not
heed those who would destroy our dreams by saying unkind
words or criticizing us—trying to pop our bubble so we stumble.

God sent us Jesus so we would be delivered from these
evils. Now, as His children, we must rise above these insults
upon what God has given us. Be of courage to overcome these
negative people in our lives. Winston Churchill stated,
"Courage is the first of human qualities because it is the quality which guarantees all the others."

Today's Action

♦ Don't listen to those who want to destroy your dreams.
Let God give you courage to overcome negative people.

Prayer

*Father God, thank You for giving me courage to overcome the
fears of the world. Amen.*

The Gift

For all things come from Thee, and from Thy hand we have given Thee.

—1 Chronicles 29:14

————◇————

I magine what a heavy schedule of appointments President Abraham Lincoln had to keep day after day. Yet when an elderly woman with no official business in mind asked to see him, he graciously consented.

As she entered Lincoln's office, he rose to greet her and asked how he might be of service. She replied that she had not come to ask a favor. She had heard that the president liked a certain kind of cookie, so she had baked some for him and brought them to his office.

With tears in his eyes, Lincoln responded, "You are the very first person who has ever come into my office asking not, expecting not, but rather bringing me a gift. I thank you from the bottom of my heart."

I know I get so excited when my children come to me with a gift, not a request. How much more must God rejoice when we don't bring a list of requests but instead we simply bring Him the gift of our gratitude and love. Nothing pleases our heavenly Father more than our sincere thanksgiving.

Today in your prayer time concentrate on the sacrifice of praise, thinking of all God's mercies to us and blessing His holiness.

Today's Action

◆ Give the gift of praise to our heavenly Father who is the giver of all good gifts.

Prayer

Father God, I just want to let You know that I'm thankful for all You do for me and my family. Amen.

The Sky's the Limit

*Grow in the grace and knowledge of our Lord
and Savior Jesus Christ.*

—2 Peter 3:18

❏
❏
❏

———◇———

Even though I played a lot of basketball in high school and college, I find today's players awesome. In my day, a six-foot guard, a six-foot forward, and a six-five center were about what you would expect a starting line-up to exhibit. Today there are many six-eight guards that dribble with the ease and finesse of a much smaller player of old. When it comes to determining how tall we might become, we must depend on our inherited genetic factors. Regardless of what we do, we stop growing at a certain height. We have a predetermined height.

However, our potential for spiritual growth is uninhibited. The sky's the limit. We can grow as tall spiritually as we want. In order to grow spiritually we must exercise our faith regularly, read God's Word regularly, and obey His teachings. When we draw close to God, He will produce a likeness to Christ in us.

Today's Action
♦ Step out today in faith, trusting the Lord to help and guide you.

Prayer
Father God, take my heart and my hands and help me grow. I want to be a spiritual giant. Amen.

Lincoln's Road to the White House

Failed in business in 1831.

Defeated for legislature in 1832.

Second failure in business in 1833.

Suffered nervous breakdown in 1836.

Defeated for speaker in 1838.

Defeated for elector in 1840.

Defeated for congress in 1843.

Defeated for congress in 1848.

Defeated for senate in 1855.

Defeated for vice president in 1856.

Defeated for senate in 1858.

Elected president in 1860.

You Have a Story to Tell

My tongue is the pen of a ready writer.

—Psalm 45:1

———◇———

In one of Charles Wesley's great hymns he wrote, "O for a thousand tongues to sing my great Redeemer's praise!" What a magnificent choir that would be—to stand in a great gathering of men to hear them sing with bellowing voices this great song of praise.

Wouldn't it be great to have 1,000 men who would be willing to be ready writers for God and all of His mercies? Each year Emilie and I have the privilege to go to the Christian Booksellers Association (CBA) Convention. As we walk the huge convention center floor we literally see aisle after aisle of books written by authors who have a story to tell. A tongue devoted to God can accomplish much. Joni Eareckson Tada, who is confined to a wheelchair and has great physical disabilities, has spoken and written to hundreds of thousands of people. She often states, "With God, less is more." Use your tongue to tell others how God has impacted your life. We all have a story to tell. We can tell it through word of mouth or through the written word.

Today's Action

◆ Tell or write to someone today and let that person know how God has made a difference in your life.

Prayer

Father God, help me to tell others about Your love and goodness. Amen.

Disconnected

He who has ears to hear, let him hear.

—Mark 4:9

❏
❏
❏

————◇————

As we move into the technology mode of life, we have many new tools to help us communicate with each other. We feel the need to go faster and faster. What was good enough for yesterday is too slow for today.

For a long time everyone kept telling me I had to have a fax machine. Finally I broke down and bought one. I can truly say I don't know how I lived without it. Occasionally, however, I do have a glitch when my incoming calls are interrupted and the message says, "Communication error, line disconnected during reception."

This has been a reminder to me of the many times I send my requests to God. He is always there to receive them—but that's not true when it comes to me receiving His messages. Often I don't want to hear what He wants me to hear. I just disconnect and post "communication error."

Today is a good day to get a service man out to debug the system to prevent any more disconnects.

Today's Action
- ◆ Give God your undivided attention and listen carefully to what He is trying to say to you.

Prayer
Father God, since You gave me two ears to hear, may I listen patiently for Your voice. Amen.

Eternal Dividends

*Beware, and be on your guard against every
form of greed; for not even when one has an
abundance does his life consist of his possessions.*

*One's life does not consist in the abundance of
the things he possesses.* (NKJV)

—Luke 12:15

———◇———

Afavorite bumper sticker displayed in Southern California is: "He Who Dies with the Most Toys Wins." And
some men believe this! I'm not saying we can't have a nice car,
home, boat, plane, ATV, water skis, or other possessions. But if
these things are what drives us to meaning, in time we will be
disappointed. Possessions by themselves will not give meaning to life.

In Luke 12:16-21 Jesus tells a parable about a man who
spent his life gathering more and more wealth, but he had no
time for God. He was a man of great wealth, but he was bankrupt in death.

We need to invest our lives in activities that pay eternal
dividends. One of the great financial principles of this world is
called "compounded interest." The compound interest charts
show overwhelming growth of principle when we continue to
invest in our account and reinvest the interest. That same principle works great in the Christian world. If we invest in eternal things of value, the Lord will bless us with abundance.

Today's Action

 ◆ Think about this question: "Where is your treasure?"

Prayer

*Father God, make me sensitive to the value of possessions. When
I want one more toy remind me to ask, "Will it give eternal value?"
Amen.*

"I Quit!"

And let us not lose heart in doing good, for in due time we shall reap if we do not grow weary.

—Galatians 6:9

❑
❑
❑

---◇---

As we look around at our jobs, churches, neighborhoods, and social gatherings, we observe people who seem to have it all. In many cases we see nonbelievers who seem to get all the breaks in life. We try to do all the right things, but life just isn't working for us. At times we yell, "What's the use? I quit!"

Perseverance and endurance are character qualities that aren't a lot of fun to acquire. In order to get them we have to be long in suffering—and that's hard. If you are facing hopeless circumstances in your life, don't give up. God promises that if we don't give up, if we plant good seeds and good deeds, we will obtain good results in time. By this faith, keep up good works. Keep on going. Be not weary in serving; do your best for those in need.

Today's Action
♦ Do one more good deed for someone who seems to have no hope.

Prayer
Father God, today I rekindle my faith. Help me do my best when I assist others. Amen.

On Trial for God

Greater is He who is in you than he who is in the world.

—1 John 4:4

---◇---

As we survey the world we begin to think that our situation is no better than in the times of the prophet Habakkuk in the year 607 B.C. In Habakkuk 1:4 we read, "The law is ignored and justice is never upheld. For the wicked surround the righteous; therefore justice comes out perverted." As I read the daily headlines I shake my head at the verdicts that are rendered in our court system. Our justice system is literally paralyzed.

Recently I had a fearful dream that Emilie and I were on trial for doing good. I woke up in a sweat because I was so shaken. As I lay there in a daze, I recounted my dream to Emilie. We both expressed a concern that someday in America that could be true.

Martyrs throughout history have died for believing in good. We often say that we would die for God, but are we willing to live for Him? First John 4:4 gives us the assurance that Jesus, who is in you, is greater than Satan, the prince of this world (see John 12:31; 14:30; Ephesians 6:12).

Today's Action

- ◆ Let us live for God today. Take a stand if the opportunity presents itself.

Prayer

Father God, give me the desire not only to die for You, but to live for You each day. Amen.

You never get promoted when no one else knows your current job. The best basis for being advanced is to organize yourself out of every job you're put in. Most people are advanced because they're pushed up from people underneath them rather than pulled by the top.

—*Donald David*

Heaven on Earth?

This is my comfort in my affliction, that Thy word has revived me.

—Psalm 119:50

❑
❑
❑

———◇———

Many religious teachers have altered the gospel by teaching that after you become a Christian the rest of your life will be similar to living in heaven. Somehow you will become wealthy, healthy, and wise—and nothing bad will happen to you. However, this is not what the Bible says will happen. All through history God-fearing believers have been caught in circumstances that are indescribable: war, famine, death, torture, and so on.

I have found that God doesn't always lift us out of our circumstances. Usually He comes into our situation. Jesus becomes the light within our darkness. In Hebrews 11:35-38 we are told that many believers often suffer. God never promises earthly perfection, but He does promise to always stand beside us and never forsake us (see Deuteronomy 31:6; Hebrews 13:5). He will give us strength and the grace to rejoice while we are in these situations.

Today's Action

♦ Ask Jesus to bring His light into your darkness.

Prayer

Father God, thank You for not letting me fear the darkness that surrounds me sometimes. I know You are with me, and You will give me real peace. Amen.

No Condemnation

For I will be merciful to their iniquities, and I will remember their sins no more.

—Hebrews 8:12

———◇———

How often have we heard and read that God not only forgives, but He also forgets. Today's verse says that God will remember our iniquities *no more.*

Paul writes in Romans 8:1: "There is therefore now no condemnation for those who are in Christ Jesus." With this great promise we are able to boldly approach His throne and confess our sins directly to Him, knowing He will not only forgive, but will remember them no more. What a tremendous promise to us!

Even though we are forgiven many times, we still have to face the consequences of our actions. Even as we suffer the results of our sins, we need to ask for and accept God's forgiveness. Then we can enjoy the beauty of the future.

Today's Action

- ◆ Thank God for His complete forgiveness of sins past, present, and future.

Prayer

Father God, thank You for remembering my sins no more. Amen.

Just Ask

What do you want Me to do for you?

—Mark 10:51

❑
❑
❑

————◇————

W hen my two children hesitated to ask me for something, I would tell them, "The worst I can say is no." My son, Brad, didn't seem to take advantage of this guideline, but Jenny, my daughter, soon learned to ask for everything. She accepted the reasoning that the worst answer I could give would be no. The odds were in her favor that I would say yes more often than no.

Throughout Scripture there are illustrations that tell us we are to ask:

- ◆ King Ahasuerus asked Queen Esther, "What is your petition? It will be given you. What is your request?" (Esther 7:2 NIV).

- ◆ Solomon prayed for an understanding heart to discern between good and evil, and "the Lord was pleased that Solomon had asked for this" (1 Kings 3:10).

- ◆ Jesus asked the blind man, "What do you want Me to do for you?" (Mark 10:51).

God is waiting for us to express our desires. Often we don't have because we don't ask. Instead of approaching God with a small coffee mug, let's expand our faith and boldly go to Him with a big ice-tea pitcher.

Today's Action

- ◆ Ask God for something that would please Him, but would overwhelm you if He answered yes. Keep praying about it.

Prayer

Father God, I make my requests knowing You care about me, and You hear me. Thank You for being such a loving Father. Amen.

The Foundation for Marriage

What therefore God has joined together, let no man separate.

—Mark 10:9

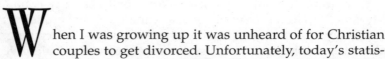

When I was growing up it was unheard of for Christian couples to get divorced. Unfortunately, today's statistic of Christian marriages ending in divorce equals that of the secular element, which is now nearing the 60 percent level. What's gone wrong? Where have we lost our focus and commitment in marriage?

Dietrich Bonhoeffer, the great German pastor killed in a German prison camp in World War II, wrote a book entitled *Letters and Papers from Prison*. In this reflection of life, he writes a wedding sermon and makes several points that should be stressed in our day of "chipped" marriages.

- ◆ God is guiding.
- ◆ God makes the union indissoluble.
- ◆ God lays on marriage both blessing (children) and burden (caring and providing for the family).
- ◆ Christ is the foundation of a marriage.

These are the building blocks for a successful marriage.

Today's Action

◆ Using these four points, how are you doing individually and as a couple? Move to strengthen your weak areas.

Prayer

Father God, may I be sensitive to those areas that need more effort on my part. Amen.

Express Your Love

*Husbands, love your wives, just as Christ also
loved the church and gave Himself up for it.*

—Ephesians 5:25

————◇————

Times have changed from commands of Scripture to feelings of Scripture. I so often hear the expression, "I don't feel like I love my husband/my wife anymore. All the feeling has left my marriage." In today's verse, nowhere do we find, "Husbands, feel like you love your wives." God, through Paul, commands: "Husbands, love your wives." It seems quite clear that we are to daily commit ourselves to loving our wives. How are we to do that? That is the $64,000 question. There are no pat formulas because each wife has her own language of love. We must be students of our wives. We must know what makes them tick and what makes them ticked. With Emilie I know that she will respond positively when I—

- give her a compliment about her appearance.
- put my arms around her and tell her that I love her.
- am considerate to her by pulling her chair out in a restaurant and opening the car door as she gets in and out.
- want to spend time with her doing what she likes to do.
- give her assurances of my love.
- don't make extra work for her to do because of my sloppiness.

Today's Action

- Do something for your wife that expresses your love for her.

Prayer

Father God, give my heart the desire to really love my wife. Help me choose each day to love her. Amen.

What Is Home?

A roof to keep out the rain. Four walls to keep out the wind. Floors to keep out the cold. Yes, but home is more than that. It is the laugh of a baby, the song of a mother, the strength of a father. Warmth of loving hearts, light from happy eyes, kindness, loyalty, comradeship.

Home is first school and first church for young ones, where they learn what is right, what is good, and what is kind. Where they go for comfort when they are hurt or sick. Where joy is shared and sorrow eased. Where fathers and mothers are respected and loved. Where children are wanted. Where the simplest food is good enough for kings because it is earned. Where money is not so important as loving-kindness. Where even the teakettle sings from happiness. That is home. God bless it.

—*Ernestine Schuman-Heink*

An Attitude of Prayer

Be anxious for nothing, but in everything by prayer and supplication with thanksgiving let your requests be made known to God.

—Philippians 4:6

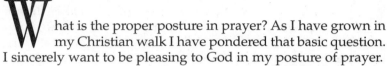

What is the proper posture in prayer? As I have grown in my Christian walk I have pondered that basic question. I sincerely want to be pleasing to God in my posture of prayer.

In searching Scripture I began to realize that there is great liberty given to praying people. The important issue is that our hearts are in communication with God. In the Scriptures we discover many "attitudes" of prayer:

- kneeling (1 Kings 8:54; Ezra 9:5; Daniel 6:10; Acts 20:36)
- standing (Jeremiah 18:20)
- sitting (2 Samuel 7:18)
- lying prostrate (Ezekiel 11:13)
- in bed (Psalm 63:6)
- in private (Matthew 6:6; Mark 1:35)
- with others (Psalm 35:18)
- anywhere (I Timothy 2:8)
- silently (1 Samuel 1:13)
- loudly (Acts 16:25)
- for everything (Genesis 24:12-14; Philippians 4:6; 1 Timothy 2:1,2)
- at all times (Luke 18:1)

Today's Action

- Within the next week try several different physical positions as you pray. Read the Scripture that goes with each.

Prayer

Father God, help me remember that You are not as concerned with my posture as You are with my daily communication. Amen.

The Power of Gentleness

*We proved to be gentle among you, as a nursing
mother tenderly cares for her own children.*

—1 Thessalonians 2:7

————◇————

One of the great compliments we can receive is that of
being gentle. Often we think that isn't so macho; however, Paul, Silvanus, and Timothy were compassionate, spiritual mentors to the Thessalonian church. These were very
rugged men who, according to Scripture, were gentle.
Although they exhibited this trait, they also exhorted, com-
forted, and admonished the Thessalonians as a father does to
his children (1 Thessalonians 2:11).

While raising my children I considered myself a very strict
father; however, my daughter recently commented that she
considered me very gentle. That was a surprise to me. I want
to be known as gentle, but I often don't feel like I respond in a
gentle way. We need gentleness when we teach our children
how to reflect God's glory. Then, in the lives of our children—
and their children—we can rejoice when we see where they
are spiritually. They are all in the growth process.

A prominent pastor once stated, "Those who minister the
gospel should be gentle, tender, and affectionate....What is
wrong we should oppose, but it should be in the kindest manner toward those who do wrong. We are to hate the sin, but
love the sinner."

Today's Action

♦ Let's apply gentleness toward others today and discover
the power of gentleness.

Prayer

*Father God, may others see me as gentle—but tough when I need
to be. Amen.*

A "Breaking-Up" Process

Consider it all joy...when you encounter various trials, knowing that the testing of your faith produces endurance.

—James 1:2,3

❑
❑
❑

———————◇———————

Many times we attempt to acquire a godly trait without first taking the time to properly prepare the soil of our lives. As a young man growing up I learned through rough experiences on the farm how difficult it was to prepare the soil. On our farm we had a lot of rocks, and we had to remove them with a lot of hard work and sweat in order to get topsoil decent for planting seeds. This process certainly taught me to have endurance and patience. God prepares the soil of our hearts to receive His Word through a "breaking up" process.

It may come through a disaster like an earthquake, a tornado, a tidal wave, a fire, or a flood. Often it comes through tragedy, sickness, a friend's death, or a disappointment. If you find yourself in the midst of hard circumstances, God may be softening or breaking up the rocks in your soil so that the seed of His Word can teach you. Often, as men, we fight this soil preparation. We want to be in control. But we need to relax and let go, to stop fighting. We need to allow God to have His way.

Today's Action
- ◆ Evaluate your situations. If you are in the midst of life-changing events, let go.

Prayer
Father God, thank You for loving me enough to change me into who You want me to become. Amen.

Surviving Hard Times

Do not fret because of evildoers.

❏
❏
❏

—Psalm 37:1

————◇————

As I look about me in life, on radio, on TV, and on the Internet I see five ways we can return to God's design and purpose. In Psalm 37, David tells us not to fret in hard situations but to:

- ◆ *trust God* (verse 3): Many times people will disappoint us but God never will.
- ◆ *do good things* (verse 3): The more good we do, the less chance that evil can make an impact.
- ◆ *delight in the Lord* (verse 4): Take delight in the things of the Lord. He promises to meet our needs.
- ◆ *Commit your way to God* (verse 5): He will be a blessing unto you.
- ◆ *Wait patiently for the Lord* (verse 7): He will overcome every situation.

The more time we spend studying God's Word and spending time with positive influences, the less time we have to worry.

Today's Action

- ◆ Look around until you find something good happening—then rejoice! Shout from the mountain top those things that are good.

Prayer

Father God, I thank You for all Your goodness. I want to grow so close to You that I don't have time for the negative. Amen.

The Promise of Forgiveness

Who is a God like Thee, who pardons iniquity?

—**Micah 7:18**

❏
❏
❏

---◇---

Somehow the church hasn't done a good job of letting the world know that churches are for sinners more than for saints. Have you ever wondered how God could forgive your sins and all of your unrighteousness toward Him? Only through the wonder of God's grace can we begin to realize the awesomeness of forgiveness. Even though we can't understand this grace, we can sit back, rejoice, and marvel at God's goodness for making us clean before Him. Micah, the great prophet, acknowledges the Lord's goodness and expresses confidence in God's continuing promise to forgive and bless His people. He was given this revelation long before Jesus came as a child, lived for 33 years, died on the cross, then rose from the grave. Micah wasn't able to read of Paul's triumphant promises of God's grace: No sin is so great that it cannot be forgiven. May we grasp this promise!

Today's Action

◆ Go to the throne of God and ask for His abundant grace that will forgive all of your sins.

Prayer

Father God, I'm thankful that I can pray in confidence and adoration declaring, "Who is a God like You!" Amen.

Throw away all ambition beyond that of doing the day's work well. The travelers on the road to success live in the present, heedless of taking thought for the morrow. Live neither in the past nor in the future, but let each day's work absorb your entire energies, and satisfy your widest ambition.

—*William Osler*

That's My Dad!

Grandchildren are the crown of old men, and the glory of sons is their fathers.

—Proverbs 17:6

❏
❏
❏

————◇————

What a great thrill it is to hear my children say with honor, "This is my dad." One of the Ten Commandments says that we are to honor our mothers and fathers (Exodus 20:12). We live in a time when many children and fathers don't honor each other. I can't think of a more wasted life than to have children and grandchildren who don't honor their father and grandfather. If this were true for me, I would rightly think that somewhere along the way I made some bad choices. Oh, yes there are some children who show irreverence to parents unjustifiably, but mainly children reflect back to us how we have behaved toward them.

A good test of whether you are a father who is respected by his children is to ask yourself, "Do I want my son or daughter to grow up and be like me?"

One way we as Christians need to be a spiritual witness to the world is through the ways our families are different—that we reflect respect and honor for others.

Today's Action

◆ Begin investing in the lives of your children today. Determine that your children will be proud to call you "dad."

Prayer

Father God, thank You for my children. Help me make a positive impact upon their lives. Amen.

An Amazing Pronouncement

Behold, Lord, half of my possessions I will give to the poor, and if I have defrauded anyone of anything, I will give back four times as much.

—Luke 19:8

———◇———

Americans are known around the world for being a generous people. Since the founding of this country, Christians have given plentifully of their wealth to build schools, hospitals, universities, medical research centers, and churches. Recent surveys indicate that evangelical Christians give more of their money to help others than any other segment of our society.

Zaccheus, a short tax man, shinnied up a sycamore tree to get a good look at Jesus. Through this encounter Zacchaeus made the revolutionary statement in today's Scripture. This is an amazing pronouncement. Have you ever encountered the truth and went away wanting to do some great act of generosity? Well, that's how this tax man felt.

How a man feels about his money usually reflects his walk with God. Show me a stingy man, and I will show you a man who is far away from God. But show me a giving man, and I'll show you someone who walks close to God.

Today's Action

♦ Do you show a love and generosity that is compatible with God's unending grace to you? Do something today to show that love.

Prayer

Father God, thank You for paying my debt on the cross and setting me free. Amen.

Beyond the Comfort Zone

He felt compassion for them, because they were distressed and downcast like sheep without a shepherd.

—Matthew 9:36

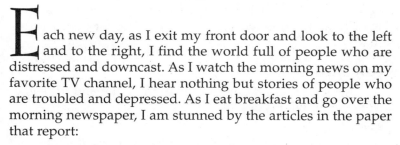

Each new day, as I exit my front door and look to the left and to the right, I find the world full of people who are distressed and downcast. As I watch the morning news on my favorite TV channel, I hear nothing but stories of people who are troubled and depressed. As I eat breakfast and go over the morning newspaper, I am stunned by the articles in the paper that report:

- ◆ Tens of thousands of Brazilians toil in bondage
- ◆ Boy six years old arrested for assaulting a month-old baby
- ◆ Gunman caught after killing 33
- ◆ Apartment fire leaves 12 dead
- ◆ Bus bombed in protest of election; 15 dead

After reading these depressing headlines, it's hard for me to finish eating breakfast. Yes, the world is full of people who are distressed and downcast.

In our passage from Matthew we find Jesus teaching in all the cities and villages and proclaiming the good news of the gospel. As He looked at the multitudes He felt compassion for them. Yet in today's culture of violence we've become desensitized to all the bad news we see, read, and hear. If it doesn't affect us and our friends, we have a tendency to turn our heads and look the other way. Maybe, instead of looking to the left and to the right, we should look upward *toward* God and utter a prayer for those people caught in distress.

We can't always do something for people in foreign countries who face terrible problems, but we can find people close to us in similar situations. Ask God to show you people you can help who face such dilemmas.

As Jesus showed compassion to those around Him, we too should show compassion. John Andrew Holmes is credited with saying, "There is no exercise better for the heart than reaching down and lifting people up." This could mean sharing a basket of food, paying a utility bill, making a phone call of encouragement, babysitting while the person looks for a job, or writing a note saying you are praying for your friend's situation.

Today's Action

- ◆ Let's go beyond our comfort zone today and lift someone up who is down!

Prayer

Father God, I know I can't reach everyone who is distressed and downcast, but let me help those around me. Amen.

No Job Is Too Small

He who is faithful in a very little thing is faithful also in much. . . .

—Luke 16:10

———◇———

We are so concerned about the kind of jobs God gives us: "Is it important enough for me?" "He certainly wouldn't want me to just empty wastebaskets, mow the lawn, wash the church bus, or type the weekly bulletin." Yet Christians who attend to these details make valuable contributions to the ministry of Christ. We must not become weary doing the little things because in God's eyes they are very important. This story illustrates my point:

> As construction began on a magnificent cathedral, the archbishop in charge promised a large reward to the person who made the most important contribution to finishing the sanctuary. As the building went up, people speculated about who would win the prize. The architect? The contractor? The artisans skilled in gold, iron, brass, and glass? Perhaps the carpenter assigned to the detailed grillwork? Because each workman did his best, the completed church was a masterpiece. When the moment came to announce the winner, everyone was surprised. It was given to an old, poorly dressed peasant woman. What had she done? Everyday she had faithfully carried hay to the ox that pulled the marble for the stonecutter.

If it's done for the Lord there is no such thing as a small task.

Today's Action

♦ Begin to help today. If you are already serving, be renewed by your contribution to the total program.

Prayer

Father God, help me be faithful in my service. Amen.

Onward and Upward

Forgetting what lies behind and reaching for-
ward to what lies ahead, I press on toward the
goal for the prize of the upward call of God in
Christ Jesus.

—Philippians 3:13,14

————◇————

We waste so much energy looking back. Oh yes, reflection is good for remembering family times together: picnics, Thanksgiving, Christmas, and other fun gatherings, but usually we dwell on the negatives.

We can't do anything about the past or future, we can only take care of today. Each of us must strive today to improve tomorrow. When Emilie and I finish a new book that is better than the last, we begin gathering data and material for that next unknown—a book that will be even better than the previous ones. We recognize that it's always possible to do a better job. We never assume we have arrived. We keep pressing onward and upward.

Looking back often leads to a feeling of complacency. Yesterday's accomplishments don't count. It's what we do today that's important. We should determine to excel for Christ so that we'll always improve—our best work is still ahead!

Today's Action

◆ Write several short-term goals (six months or less) for your life. Be sure to stretch yourself.

Prayer

Father God, thank You for challenging me to grow in my faith and not to become complacent. Amen.

I know Christ dwells within me all the time, guiding me and inspiring me whenever I do or say anything. A light of which I caught no glimmer before comes to me at the very moment when it is needed.

—*Saint Therese of Lisieux*

Rise Up!

He said to the paralytic, "I say to you, rise, and take up your stretcher and go home."

—Luke 5:24

——◇——

I n our Scripture study today we see several strands of truth. The passage opens with some friends of a crippled man who want to bring him to Jesus to be healed.

The sick man couldn't walk, so they carried him on his personal bed. Can you imagine how the people of the city stared as they watched a man being carried on his bed to see Jesus? As the group arrived at the house where Jesus was teaching, they saw a large crowd of people. They couldn't even get close enough to Jesus to ask for the healing of their friend.

So one of the friends said, "Let's go over the crowd and take him up on the rooftop." They climbed up some outside stairs with the sick man on his bed. They discussed taking off some of the flat roof so they could lower the man and his bed inside the house near Jesus. I can just hear the dialogue that went on between the friends:

- ◆ This will be fun—like a party.
- ◆ We can't tear into a roof!
- ◆ The debris will fall down on top of Jesus.
- ◆ Who will fix the roof when we're finished?

Fortunately for the sick man, someone took control and started removing a section of the roof. Then the group tied ropes to the corners of the bed and lowered the man and his bed through the hole in the roof.

You can imagine the amazement that Jesus and those in the crowd experienced when they saw a man and a bed being lowered through the roof:

- ◆ The nerve of them!
- ◆ Can't they wait their turn?
- ◆ Gate-crashers!
- ◆ Escort them out!
- ◆ They must truly believe!

Jesus looked at the man who had come down through the roof. Then He smiled and said, "Your sins are forgiven."

The friends didn't waste time by debating who would fix the roof. They just earnestly wanted to get their friend healed and did what was necessary. Jesus also was open to the very unorthodox way the sick man was brought to Him. The sick man was obedient to Jesus' command when He said, "Rise...and go home." Luke 5:25 says, "At once he rose up before them, and took up what he had been lying on, and went home glorifying God."

Today's Action

- ◆ Stand and walk to wherever Jesus is telling you to go.

Prayer

Father God, let my heart be obedient to Your command. Amen.

Passionate for Christ

> *I am not ashamed of the gospel, for it is the power of God for salvation to everyone who believes.*

> **—Romans 1:16**

———◇———

D r. R. Newton was passionate in his plea of not being ashamed of the gospel when he declared:

Ashamed of the gospel of Christ! Let the skeptic, let the wicked profligate, blush at his deeds of darkness, which will not bear the light, lest they should be made manifest; but never let the Christian blush to own the holy gospel. Where is the philosopher who is ashamed to own the God of Nature? Where is the Jew that is ashamed of Moses? Or the Moslem that is ashamed of Mahomet? And shall the Christian, and the Christian minister, be ashamed of Christ? God forbid! No! Let me be ashamed of myself, let me be ashamed of the world, and let me blush at sin; but never, ever, let me be ashamed of the gospel of Christ!

As I reflect upon my life, I have to confess that I've had an easy time sharing the gospel due to the religious climate in America over the years. Lately, however, I've begun to realize that the religious freedom of the past may not be the same freedom of the future.

In Romans 1:1-17, Paul teaches seven principles about the gospel:

- ◆ *We are all set apart for the gospel:* What an awesome thought! That makes us something special in the sight of God. With this thought, we can establish our daily priorities.

62

- *This gospel was promised beforehand through His prophets:* We must realize that this precious gospel has a historical background that has been documented in the Bible.

- *We are to share the gospel with our whole hearts:* With a passion and a zeal we are to share this good news with our friends and acquaintances.

- *We are to share the gospel with everyone:* Paul says he was obligated and eager to preach the gospel to both Greeks and nonGreeks, to the wise and to the foolish.

- *We are to take a stand for the gospel:* We should be individuals and families who stand together and exhibit a lifestyle that reflects the love of Christ.

- *We need to see the power of the gospel for salvation:* The gospel is a change agent, giving us real purpose and meaning to life—and it helps us fight the power of sin.

- *We are to live a life of righteousness by faith:* The righteousness of God is revealed in the gospel so we can go out and live a righteous life by the power of the Holy Spirit. We are to be the light of the world.

Today's Action

- Read a good biography of one of the pillars of the church who reflects the power of the gospel in his or her life. (Suggestions: Charles Spurgeon, J. Dwight Moody, Martyn Lloyd Jones, Amy Carmichael, Susanna Wesley, Corrie ten Boom.)

Prayer

Father God, thank You for my salvation. May I be bolder with my faith. Amen.

Proud to Be an American

Let every person be in subjection to the govern-ing authorities. For there is no authority except from God, and those which exist are established by God.

—Romans 13:1

————————◇————————

Never do I appreciate our government so much as when Emilie and I travel out of the United States. And when we return again to our homeland, we say, "There's no place like America."

Today's political climate and freedom means that we can be very critical of our policy makers. It is not popular to be a political leader today, not even for the president. Today's read-ing says that all governments are ordained by God. Without Him there would be no governments.

When I go into a grocery store I can be assured that the products I purchase will be healthy. When I purchase an auto-mobile I know that the brakes will work. I know that the clothes I purchase won't ignite and put me or my loved ones in flames. How do I know? Because our government has strengthened its control over the quality of products from food to perfume. Legislation has been enacted, factory inspections required, labeling standardized, and safety tests performed. This is government when it's working, and I appreciate good government at work.

Today's Action

- ◆ Let us thank God for what He has given us. Pray for our government leaders.

Prayer

Father God, thank You for making America a great country. Amen.

Wisdom from Above

Who among you is wise and understanding?
Let him show by his good behavior his deeds in
the gentleness of wisdom.

—James 3:13

❑
❑
❑

――――◇――――

I have an identical twin brother named Bill. When my children, Jennifer and Bradley, were very young they couldn't tell us apart. They addressed us as "two daddies." When our grandchildren arrived, they also were confused when we were together. They would say "two papas."

That's the way it is with wisdom. There are two types of wisdom. They come from different sources, have different means, and most definitely have different ends. James talks about these two wisdoms in chapter 3, verses 15-18:

♦ one which comes from above
♦ one which is earthly, natural, and demonic

The one that comes from above is—

♦ pure
♦ gentle
♦ peaceable
♦ reasonable
♦ full of mercy
♦ full of good fruits
♦ unwavering

The second wisdom produces—

♦ bitter jealousy
♦ selfish ambition
♦ lies against the truth
♦ arrogance

Notice the difference in the fruit that each one produces:

- The first produces the fruit of righteousness and peace
- The second produces the fruit of disorder and every evil thing

Wouldn't it be nice to have both wisdom and youth at the same time? Life, however, doesn't work that way.

Luci Swindoll says "The good life is peace—knowing that I was considerate instead of crabby, that I stood by faithfully when all the chips were down for the other guy, that I showed impartiality when I really wanted my preference, that I had the courage to deter reward for something better down the road. Why couldn't I have learned this when I still had a young body?"

Today's Action

- Step out and exercise the wisdom from above.

Prayer

Father God, let me be an easy learner regarding wisdom. I really don't want to wait for the hard knocks and suffering. Amen.

Thank God

Blessed be the LORD, *because He has heard the voice of my supplication.*

—Psalm 28:6

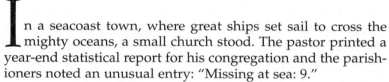

I n a seacoast town, where great ships set sail to cross the mighty oceans, a small church stood. The pastor printed a year-end statistical report for his congregation and the parishioners noted an unusual entry: "Missing at sea: 9."

The members of the congregation didn't know of any of their number who had been lost at sea, so someone asked the pastor what he meant.

"Well," he replied, "during the year, eleven of you asked me to pray for family or friends going out to sea. Because I heard only two of you thank the Lord for their safe return, I assume the remaining nine are still missing!"

We often forget to give thanks when God answers our prayers. We should be quick to show our appreciation because our heavenly Father is pleased when we thank Him.

When our Lord was on earth, He lifted His voice to His Father and expressed thanks for food (John 6:11), the simplicity of the gospel (Matthew 11:25), and answered prayer (John 11:41).

Today's Action

◆ Thank God for answered prayers.

Prayer

Father God, I thank You over and over again for Your goodness and provision. Amen.

I'm drinking from the saucer
If God gives me strength and courage,
When the way grows steep and rough,
I'll not ask for any other blessings—
I'm already blessed enough.
May I never be too busy,
To help bear another's load.
I'm drinking from the saucer,
'Cause my cup has overflowed!

—Author unknown

A Basket of Thoughts

"For My thoughts are not your thoughts, neither are your ways My ways," declares the LORD.

—Isaiah 55:8

❏
❏
❏

———◇———

Suppose a man should find a great basket by the wayside, carefully packed, and upon opening it he discovered it was filled with human thoughts—all the thoughts that had passed through one single brain in one year. What a medley they would make! How many thoughts would be wild and foolish, how many weak and contemptible, how many mean and vile, how many so contradictory and crooked they could hardly lie still in the basket? And suppose the man should be told that these were all his *own* thoughts, the children of his own brain? How amazed he would be—and how little prepared to see himself as revealed in those thoughts! I'm sure he would want to run away and hide if all the world looked into the open basket and saw his thoughts!

Compared to the thoughts of God, we humans seem so frail. I can't imagine having the lowliness of my thoughts exposed. I'm sometimes amazed that I even think of such things. At times I ask, "God, why did You permit that plane crash?" or "Why was it necessary for that murder to take place?" At times I want to crawl inside God's mind and see how it functions and how He thinks. Then I realize that He is the potter, and I am the clay. His thoughts are so much higher than mine.

In Philippians 4:8, Paul gives us some idea of God's thought process. He tells us to think on these things:

- ◆ whatever is true
- ◆ whatever is honorable

- whatever is right
- whatever is pure
- whatever is lovely
- whatever is of good repute
- if there is any excellence and if anything worthy of praise, let your mind dwell on these things

As Christians, we are models that people watch to see what godly life is about. Either they accept our level of thought, or they reject it by what they have learned, received, heard, and seen in us.

Today's Action

- Examine your thought life. How does it compare to Philippians 4:8?

Prayer

Father God, help me become more aware of what is excellent and worthy of praise. I want my mind to dwell on these things. Amen.

Governed by Love

*But take care lest this liberty of yours somehow
become a stumbling block to the weak.*

—1 Corinthians 8:9

❑
❑
❑

————◇————

Often I'm asked: "What are the minimum daily requirements for being a Christian?" "How much should I
pray?" "How much should I give?"

Paul discusses the question of whether Christians can eat
meat offered to the idols of pagan gods. God's Word gave him
an okay sign, but for Paul to do what was permitted would
put him on a course that could hurt or even destroy a weaker
Christian. In dealing with his conscience, he stopped eating
the meat.

Do you ever face the same dilemma? Do you choose not
do something that is permissible because, but for the love of a
new Christian, you don't want to be a stumbling block to his
or her walk with the Lord? Paul chose not to insist on his own
rights. He realized that liberty must be controlled and gov-
erned by love. This is a basic principle we must live by because
a fellow believer might act contrary to his own conscience
based on how he sees us live. When we love the Lord, we will
also love our brother. Love does limit liberty to promote the
maturing of our Christian brothers.

Today's Action

◆ Are any of your liberties hindering your brother from
maturing in the Lord? If so, consider how you can
change—then do it.

Prayer

*Father God, help me examine my actions and evaluate my liber-
ties so I can love my brother or sister more. Amen.*

71

Fighting Dissonance

That Christ may dwell in your hearts through faith; and that you, being rooted and grounded in love, may be able to comprehend. . .what is the breadth and length and height and depth, and to know the love of Christ. . . .

—Ephesians 3:17-19

————————◇————————

A traveler in Germany saw an unusual sight in a tavern where he stopped for dinner. After the meal, the land-lord put a great dish of soup on the floor and gave a loud whistle. Into the room came a big dog, a large cat, an old raven, and a very large rat with a bell about its neck. All four went to the dish and, without disturbing each other, ate together. After they had eaten, the dog, the cat, and the rat lay before the fire, while the raven hopped around the room. These animals had been well trained by the landlord. Not one of them tried to hurt any of the others. The traveler's comment was, that if a dog, a rat, a cat, and a bird can learn to live hap-pily together, little children—even brothers and sisters—ought to be able to do the same.

Sadly, however, families are too often characterized by disharmony. When that's the case, we do well to model our prayers for our family after Paul's words in today's reading from Ephesians. What he prays for can lead to harmony at home:

- ◆ Pray that your family may be "rooted and grounded in love" (3:17). God's love can help us be patient and kind with one another.

- ◆ Pray that each member of your family would be able to grasp "how wide and long and high and deep is the love of Christ" for him or her (3:18 NIV). Knowing Christ's immeasurable love for us, knowing that He loves us just as we are, knowing that He made us special and unique, and knowing that He died for our sins enables us to love one another.

♦ Pray that each family member would "know the love of Christ which surpasses knowledge" (3:19). Because of our human limitations, we cannot fully comprehend God's love for us.

♦ Pray that each member of your family will "be filled up to all the fulness of God" (3:19).

Each day as I read God's Word, I learn more about His patience, mercy, forgiveness, joy, justice, kindness, and compassion—the list goes on and on. Can you imagine being filled completely with these characteristics of God? Can you imagine each member of your family being filled with these qualities? What a wonderful place your home would be! And that is what Christian life is all about.

Today's Action

♦ Show each member of your family that you love them.

Prayer

Father God, I earnestly pray that You would work in my family's hearts to root and establish us in love. Amen.

No Visas Required

———————◇———————

Many years ago, when I was in the manufacturing business, Emilie and I had the privilege of going on an awards trip to Spain and North Africa with approximately 100 dealers and their wives. What a thrilling experience. We applied for our passports and visas and, in about four weeks, we were cleared to take this great adventure. While in Spain we traveled on May first, which is a sometimes turbulent "labor day" for that country. Wherever we went we were met with guards carrying automatic rifles. They anticipated possible rioting and were very careful when they inspected our paperwork to make sure everything was in order.

The next day we sailed to Algiers, North Africa, where the immigration authorities came around and requested that we drop our passports and visas into a bag so they could clear us as a group. Emilie and I were very hesitant to do this because our passports were our proof of American citizenship. We were very grateful when they were returned with the proper stamps.

It won't be like that when we enter heaven. Christians are honored citizens there. When our time comes, we won't have to worry if we get in. No guards, no passports, no visas, and no border crossings. We'll be welcomed into heaven because our citizenship papers are already there.

Today's Action

♦ Make sure that your citizenship in heaven is assured.

Prayer

Lord Jesus, I really appreciate what You did on the cross so I can gain access to heaven. Amen.

A Father's Job

Fathers, do not provoke your children to anger;
but bring them up in the discipline and instruc-
tion of the Lord.

—Ephesians 6:4

⟨⟩

Last night my little boy confessed to me
Some childish wrong;
And kneeling at my knee,
He prayed with tears—
"Dear God, make me a man
Like Daddy—wise and strong;
I know you can."

Then while he slept
I knelt beside his bed,
Confessed my sins,
And prayed with low-bowed head—
"O God, make me a child
Like my child here—
Pure, guileless,
Trusting Thee with faith sincere."

—Andrew Gillies

Too often we men have delegated the job of training our children to our wives. However, Paul is quite clear when he states that fathers have this responsibility. When we do teach our kids, we need to ask ourselves, "What is the best way to do this?" Psalm 78 gives us some help in making sure we are training our children properly.

One way we can do this is by telling "the generation to come the praises of the LORD" (verse 4). When we share our

75

praises with our children, they will see by our words and testimony that we are Christians (see verses 6,7).

Deuteronomy 6:7 says that we are to diligently teach our children when we talk, when we sit down, when we walk, when we lie down, and when we rise up. In other words, at all times we are to be on the alert for teaching opportunities.

Today's Action

- ◆ Decide that you are going to take more responsibility for teaching your children about God—and follow through.

Prayer

Father God, thank You for giving me the responsibility to teach my children. It has been so gratifying. Amen.

If a child lives with criticism, he learns to condemn.

If a child lives with hostility, he learns to fight.

If a child lives with fears, he learns to be apprehensive.

If a child lives with pity, he learns to be happy for himself.

If a child lives with encouragement, he learns to be confident.

If a child lives with tolerance, he learns to be patient.

If a child lives with praise, he learns to be appreciative.

If a child lives with acceptance, he learns to love.

If a child lives with approval, he learns to like himself.

If a child lives with recognition, he learns to have a goal.

If a child lives with fairness, he learns what justice is.

If a child lives with honesty, he learns what the truth is.

If a child lives with security, he learns to have faith in himself and in those around him.

If a child lives with friendliness, he learns that the world is
a good place in which to live.

—Author unknown

A Teachable Spirit

> *For I have chosen him, in order that he may*
> *command his children and his household after*
> *him to keep the way of the* Lord *by doing right-*
> *eousness and justice. . . .*

—Genesis 18:19

————————◇————————

Lee Iacocca in his book, *Straight Talk,* shows how he was able to balance his life in work and family. He writes,

My parents spent a lot of time with me, and I wanted my kids to be treated with as much love and care as I got. Well, that's a noble objective. Everyone feels that way. But to translate it into daily life, you really have to work at it.

There's always the excuse of work to get in the way of the family. I saw how some of the guys at Ford lived their lives—weekends merely meant two more days at the office. That wasn't my idea of family life. I spent all my weekends with the kids and all my vacations. Kathi was on the swim team for seven years, and I never missed a meet. Then there were tennis matches. I made all of them. And piano recitals. I made all of them too. I was always afraid that if I missed one, Kathi might finish first or finish last and I would hear about it secondhand and not be there to congratulate—or console—her.

People used to ask me: "How could somebody as busy as you go to all those swim meets and recitals?" I just put them down on my calendar as if I were seeing a supplier or a dealer that day. I'd write down: "Go to country club. Meet starts at 3:30, ends 4:30." And I'd zip out.

We have to make so many choices in each 24-hour day. How do we establish what's important? By reconfirming day by day what's of value to us. Our Scripture today helps us realize that as children of God we have been chosen and are directed by Him to do what is right and just.

Do you really know you have been chosen by God? What a tremendous revelation! We are living in an age of irresponsibility, but as God's children we have responsibilities. What are you doing to be directed by God? You can start by always having a teachable spirit. Each day choose to be a learner. Since we do what we want to do, ask God to direct you and show you what is right and just.

Today's Action

- ◆ Determine if God is giving you specific directions for raising your children. If so, what are they?

Prayer

Father God, thank You for choosing me to be one of Your children. I want to be a faithful steward. Amen.

The Worst Day Fishing...

———————◇———————

S t. Francis of Assisi was hoeing his garden when someone
asked what he would do if he were suddenly to learn that
he would die before sunset that very day. "I would finish hoeing my garden," he replied.

St. Francis definitely understood the worth of his hands.
We men struggle with knowing the worth of our hands. We
debate with ourselves what our work worth is: "Am I in the
right profession?" "I don't like my job; I want to change jobs
every four years." "I'm restless in what I do; I don't find fulfillment in my job." A lot of men get trapped in what they do.
A fisherman once said, "The worst day of fishing is better than
the best day at work." Our work ethic has changed tremendously from the founding days of our country. Then, a man's
work had religious significance. It was unto the Lord that he
worked. His craftsmanship reflected upon God. A man took
great pride in his end product. We need to return to that mind-
set—that our jobs are a testimony to our Savior. Can those
around us see our Jesus by the way we work? If not, that could
be the reason why we're hesitant about the worth in our
hands.

Today's Action

- ◆ If your job is drudgery to you, change your attitude
  toward it—or switch to a job that you can get excited
  about.

Prayer

*Father God, thank You for giving me hands to work. May my
work reflect my love for You. Amen.*

Better Than Sliced Bread

For by me your days will be multiplied, and
years of life will be added to you.

—Proverbs 9:11

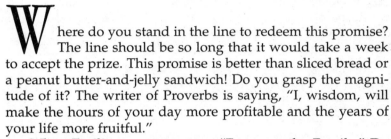

W here do you stand in the line to redeem this promise?
The line should be so long that it would take a week
to accept the prize. This promise is better than sliced bread or
a peanut butter-and-jelly sandwich! Do you grasp the magnitude of it? The writer of Proverbs is saying, "I, wisdom, will
make the hours of your day more profitable and the years of
your life more fruitful."

When Emilie was a guest on "Focus on the Family," Dr.
James Dobson shared this particular verse of Scripture. Since
the name of our ministry is "More Hours in My Day," how
appropriate this verse was. Truly God will give us more hours
in our day if we will only apply His principles to our daily
routine.

Today's Action

- ◆ Start each day with God through reading Scripture and
  prayer.
- ◆ Be anxious for nothing—give each day to the Lord.
- ◆ Be encouraging in whatever you do.
- ◆ Be in continual prayer.
- ◆ Give thanks in all things.

Prayer

Father God, I appreciate that You will give me and my family a
longer life because of our faith in You. Thank You. Amen.

Red Hearts and White Lace

But the greatest of these is love.

—1 Corinthians 13:13

———◇———

I loved Valentine's Day when I was in elementary school. I anxiously waited to receive that special red heart from a would-be girlfriend. When I did, my heart fluttered; when I didn't, I was so disappointed. I also glanced around to see how my valentines were received. This was a special day because I was learning to express love.

A few years ago, Emilie and I spoke at a Valentine's Day dinner and presented what each letter means to us:

V — Value your mate.
A — Always clear the records before nightfall.
L — Love your wife as Christ loved the church.
E — Enjoy your mate.
N — Notice her new dress, hair, and the fragrance of her perfume.
T — Teach her the work of God.
I — Invite your wife to lunch or dinner.
N — Need a friend?—ask her.
E — Exercise and grow—with your mate.

Red hearts and white lace can never convey the truth of God's love. The ultimate expression of love is found in John 3:16: "For God so loved the world, that He gave His only begotten Son, that whoever believes in Him should not perish, but have eternal life."

Today's Action

♦ Share with your wife your love for her.

Prayer

Father God, thank You for setting the standard for love. Help me share Your love with everybody. Amen.

82

A Way of Escape

For we do not have a high priest who cannot sympathize with our weaknesses, but One who has been tempted in all things as we are, yet without sin.

—Hebrews 4:15

————◇————

One of the great offerings of grace is that we can go directly to God without a high priest. We can enter into God's abode without the blood of animals and peace offerings. When Jesus walked on this earth He was tempted just like we are. He had many forks in the road that required daily decision-making in order to stay on the high road. Yes, He was a man just like us in every way but two—He never yielded to temptation, and He never fell into sin. However, He did experience the need to wait on God for guidance.

We receive some outstanding benefits from Jesus' life here on earth. When we call to Him for assistance and forgiveness in our difficult periods of life, He's always in a position to state, "Yes, I know what you're experiencing, I've been there before." He can identify with how hard it can be to live for God in this fallen world. Isn't it great to know that He has experienced what we are now experiencing? In 1 Corinthians 10:13 Paul gives us a great promise—when we are tempted, God, in His faithfulness, will give us a way to escape so we can endure it.

Today's Action

♦ When you are tempted, seek out the way to escape.

Prayer

Father God, please help me when I stumble and be merciful to me, a sinner. Amen.

It takes so little to make us glad,
Just a cheering clasp of a friendly hand,
Just a word from one who can understand;
And we finish the task we long had planned,
And we lose the doubt and the fear we had—
So little it takes to make us glad.

—*Ida Goldsmith Morris*

Entering Heaven's Gate

*Things which eye has not seen and ear has not
heard, and which have not entered the heart of
man, all that God has prepared for those who
love Him.*

—1 Corinthians 2:9

———————◇———————

Had He not made the dazzling sun
To guide us till our day's work is done,
How could we understand that Light
Which makes the Heavenly city bright.

—Sarah Lewis

Have you ever pondered what heaven might be like?
Since I was a child I've often given thought to what it
will be like after this present existence. One thing is for sure:
God, Jesus, and the Holy Spirit will be there. C.S. Lewis said
that while on this earth we are on the wrong side of the door.
But he also added, "All the leaves of the New Testament are
rustling with the rumor it will not always be so." Knowing
Jesus as our personal Savior and believing and accepting what
He did on the cross for our sins gives us entrance into eternity.
We will not enter heaven's gate because of our good character
or service. We will see our Savior only because of our faith in
His supreme sacrifice on the cross.

When we reach heaven we will truly understand today's
Scripture. The doors of heaven will be opened by God to those
who open their hearts to Him.

Today's Action

◆ Contemplate what heaven will be like.

Prayer

*Father God, prepare my heart to look forward to the day when I
will be with You in heaven. Amen.*

Entering the Unknown

*The officers ... commanded the people, saying,
"When you see the ark of the covenant of the Lord
your God ... then you shall set out from your
place and go after it. However ... do not come
near it, that you may know the way which you
shall go, for you have not passed this way before."*

—Joshua 3:2-4

———————◇———————

Some men are thrill-seekers. The faster the blood flows
through their veins, the more alive they feel. These people
live on the edge. To them, the normalcy of life is boring, so
they just make it happen.

My own style is a little more on the conservative side, so I
have a tendency to play it safe.

Many situations in life require a lot of faith on our part
because we've never "passed this way before." Unknown situations make us uneasy. But we know that talking to Christian
friends, reading Scripture, and praying will give us the
insights we need to handle difficult situations.

Joshua, much like Moses when he led the nation of Israel
out of Egypt and had to part the Red Sea, had to lead his
people across a dried-up Jordan River. The priests had never
had such a faith experience. They had to keep walking,
putting their feet into the water of the Jordan River before it
would dry up. What faith had to be exhibited!

Today's Action

- ◆ Contemplate the faith-stretching situations in your life.
  Are you depending on God for guidance? Even though
  you may not have passed this way before, have faith
  that God will see you through.

Prayer

*Father God, give me the heart to have extreme faith in extreme
situations. Amen.*

Contentment

I have learned to be content whatever the circumstances.

—Philippians 4:11b

❏
❏
❏

————◇————

C.H. Spurgeon once told of a bankrupt man who said he had been ruined by a new sofa. The man explained, "That sofa was the bad beginning—it was too fine for me. It made my old chairs and table look awful, and so I bought new ones. Then the curtains had to be replaced. The furniture in the other rooms was sold, and new articles were bought to correspond with what we had in the parlor. Soon we found that the house was not good enough for the furniture, and so we moved into a larger one. And now, here I am, bankrupt."

When Emilie and I moved into our home she said, "I can move in here and not do one thing!" *Whew*, I thought, believing her. Fifteen years and several thousand dollars later we are still fixing up our home. Although content with what we had, we wanted to develop our home's potential. In contrast, when we visited several homes of people stationed at March Air Base, we found no curtains on the windows, the rooms were sparsely decorated, and most of the moving boxes were still packed in the garage. In asking why, the lady of the house usually responds, "I can't wait for a new transfer in three years."

Contentment is being satisfied with everything you have. One of our family sayings is, "If you're not content with what you have, you will never be content with what you want."

Today's Action
◆ Try to be content in an area that has bothered you.

Prayer
Father God, thank You for all You have given me. Amen.

A True Legacy

What do these stones mean to you?

—Joshua 4:6b

❏
❏
❏

———◇———

Our country has many monuments erected so that we remember what great events took place either in a particular spot or nation-wide. We never want to let future generations forget what great sacrifices were made in order for them to have freedom.

Joshua built a monument of stones so that the children of the future would ask, "What do these stones mean?" Then the people could say to them, 'Because the waters of the Jordan were cut off before the ark of the covenant of the LORD; when it crossed the Jordan, the waters of the Jordan were cut off.' So these stones shall become a memorial to the sons of Israel forever" (verses 6,7).

As a father and grandfather, I often wonder what my legacy will be when the Lord calls me home: Will my family remember me as a man who spent his life with hay and stubble, or will they remember that I was a man of God who represented the true virtues of life? Each day I find myself continuing to make those choices that require commitment to God. I trust that my legacy will reflect the man I've tried to become.

Today's Action

♦ How would your children answer this question: "What do these 'stones' mean to you?"

Prayer

Father God, may my monument reflect that I am Your child. Amen.

The Water of Life

If any man is thirsty, let him come to Me and drink.

—John 7:37

❏
❏
❏

————◇————

tarted in southern California, but soon stretching across America, is the bottled water craze. Everywhere I go I find people carrying and drinking their personal supply of water. I've never seen so many thirsty people. We pay more for a gallon of water than we do for a gallon of gas. If we are at an outdoor event and it happens to be hot, the price goes up two- or threefold. What was common has become very expensive.

The hot books on health-stands are information on the need to drink more and more water each day. If you took the suggestions of some water advocates, you would literally float away.

In today's verse Jesus asks if anyone is thirsty. Literally, He is asking, "Does anyone need help in life? If so, come and drink what I have to offer." Many people have a difficult time admitting they need help. We really are a varied group, with our broken dreams, broken promises, fortunes that never came, homes that were never built, and marriages that never endured. Jesus says to drink from His well for righteousness. The world is thirsty for a clean conscience, a new heart, and forgiven sins. We long to be made right again.

Today's Action

- ◆ Turn to Jesus for guidance and drink from His well of righteousness.

Prayer

Father God, I am thirsty and need to daily drink from Your well. Help me turn to You. Please make me whole. Amen.

I do not ask to walk smooth paths
Nor bear an easy load.
I pray for strength and fortitude
To climb the rock-strewn road.

Give me such courage I can scale
The hardest peaks alone,
And transform every stumbling block
Into a steppingstone.

—*Gail Brook Burket*

The Book of Books

For our gospel did not come to you in word only,
but also in power.

—1 Thessalonians 1:5

❏
❏
❏

————◇————

We so take for granted our present-day Bible and its many translations. But in the first century the gospel was transmitted verbally while it was being put into written form. Believers throughout time have proclaimed the truths of Scripture around the world—even in some countries that don't take kindly to Christianity. The Bible has become the number-one bestseller because God's Word brings salvation and hope to people of every station in life.

The broad influence of this Book of books was expressed beautifully by American clergyman and author Henry van Dyke:

> Born in the East and clothed in oriental form and imagery, the Bible walks the ways of all the world with familiar feet and enters land after land to find its own everywhere. It has learned to speak in hundreds of languages to the heart of man. It comes into the palace of the monarch to tell him that he is a servant of the Most High, and into the cottage to assure the peasant that he is a child of God.

Kings and peasants have read it and believed, nations have been altered, and cultures have improved because of the Bible's message. Yes, the Bible has indeed made a difference wherever it has gone.

Men, the Scriptures can change your life if you will read it, digest the concepts, learn the truths, and apply them to your life. Great light has shown from this Book—even in the world's darkest hours.

Today's Action

- ◆ Take a moment and thank God for giving us people who have fervently and accurately translated the Bible into many languages.

Prayer

Father God, help me respect the contents of this Holy Bible and apply its precepts to my life. Amen.

The Straight Scoop

Stern discipline is for him who forsakes the way;
he who hates reproof will die.

—Proverbs 15:10

———◇———

W ho holds you accountable? We all need someone—a
wife, a pastor, a friend, a member of our church—to
whom we can pour out our deepest heartaches and thoughts.

Other than the Lord, I find my wife's input very valuable.
Over the years Emilie has helped me discern how to respond
to our children and other relationships. She is my friend, and
she is certainly on my team. I am also fortunate because I have
some male friends I've known for 30-plus years. They give me
the straight scoop. They go right to the heart of the issue,
telling me where I've been insensitive to those I love.

We all have blind spots that need illuminating. If not
exposed, they will hinder our spiritual growth. We have to
learn to accept loving, caring constructive criticism. If we
aren't accountable to another person, we may never understand why people don't feel comfortable around us.

Today's Action

◆ Go to a friend and ask him to shed light on one of your
blind spots.

Prayer

Father God, thank You for friends who will hold me accountable.
Amen.

Proclaiming Your God

And you shall write them on the doorposts of your house and on your gates.

—Deuteronomy 6:9

———◇———

S hortly after Scottish preacher G. Campbell Morgan's wedding, his father visited the home the newlyweds had just furnished and decorated. After they had shown him the place with pride and satisfaction, he remarked, "Yes, it's very nice, but no one walking through here would know whether you belong to God or the devil!"

Morgan was shocked by his father's gruff but well-meaning comment. But he got the point. From that day forward, he made certain that in every room of his home there was some evidence of their faith in Christ.

In many of Emilie's books on hospitality she shares with her readers the idea of having a welcoming plaque in their front-porch area. This gives visitors an indication that they are welcome. You can also have other reminders around the house:

- Bible verses inscribed on plaques.

- tasteful art with a Christian theme including a related Bible verse below the picture.

- have Christian books and magazines on coffee tables and in reading areas.

- worshipful selections of Christian music—instrumental and vocal.

- a blackboard near the front entrance where you can print a verse of Scripture, or jot a praise telling the whole world what God has done for you and your family. (You can also write a note to guests who are visiting. They'll love seeing their names on the blackboard announcing their welcome.)

◆ Fly Christian-related banners on your flag pole.

Changing and rearranging these reminders often keep the sentiments fresh and draw attention to the Lord we serve.

Today's Action

◆ Select one way you can signal to your guests that they are in a home that loves the Lord, then do it.

Prayer

Father God, help me be creative in sharing the gospel with others. Amen.

One Long Look

I have made a covenant with my eyes. . . .

—Job 31:1a

❏
❏
❏

———————◇———————

Job made a covenant with his eyes not to look lustfully at a woman. He is making a commitment to a special kind of blind love. He isn't saying he will never notice an attractive female because that's just not possible. There are good-looking women everywhere; men can't help seeing attractive women.

Job is saying that he might notice pretty women, but he won't lust after them. He is stating that there is a difference between a look and a stare of lust. It is said that a male student at Bob Jones University asked Bob Jones, Senior, "How often can you look at a woman before it becomes lustful?" Mr. Jones replied, "You never take two looks, but you can take one long look."

As a husband in a monogamous society we must learn to discipline our eyes. We need to train ourselves to only notice—not lustfully stare. A one-woman kind of man will avoid certain videos, magazines, movies, and television programs. We must also be willing to battle Satan when we are alone in a motel room or on the road 100 miles from home. As men we need to develop a kind of love that will put blinders on our eyes when the lust of the flesh tries to get a stronghold in our lives.

Today's Action
◆ Flee from sins of the flesh.

Prayer
Father God, put blinders on my eyes when I'm tempted to look at a woman lustfully. Amen.

Fathers and Daughters

My little daughter is at the point of death; please come and lay Your hands on her, that she may get well and live.

—Mark 5:23

————◇————

C hildren, and little girls in particular, are the nicest things that happen to people. Girls are born with a little bit of angel-shine about them, and, though it wears thin sometimes, there is always enough left to laser your heart—even when they're sitting in the mud, crying temperamental tears, or parading up the street in your wife's best clothes.

> God borrows from many creatures to make a little girl. He uses the song of a bird, the squeal of a pig, the stubbornness of a mule, the antics of a monkey, the spryness of a grasshopper, the curiosity of a cat, the speed of a gazelle, the slyness of a fox, the softness of a kitten, and to top it all off, He adds the mysterious mind of a woman.
>
> —Alan Beck

As fathers, we have a tremendous responsibility to keep our little girls on the right track. No other part of society has as much influence on our girls as we do. Our daughters want us to be the leaders of our home. She is finding in you the qualities she will someday look for in a husband. She needs to discover how a man thinks about life and how he administers and delegates certain job responsibilities to the family team.

You are the most important man in your daughter's life. She will build her life based on what she sees in you.

Today's Action

♦ Give your daughter a hug and tell her you love her.

Prayer

Father God, give me the wisdom to enrich my daughter's life. Amen.

A baby is God's opinion that life should go on. Never will a time come when the most marvelous recent invention is as marvelous as a newborn baby. The finest of our precision watches, the most supercolossal of our supercargo planes, don't compare with a newborn baby in the number and ingenuity of coils and springs, in the flow and change of chemical solutions, in timing devices and interrelated parts that are irreplaceable.

—*Carl Sandburg*

A Rich and Pleasing Intimacy

May he kiss me with the kisses of his mouth! For your love is better than wine.

—Song of Songs 1:2

———◇———

Song of Songs (Solomon) portrays the pattern of married love as God intended it to be. This dynamic Bible book is about the marriage between the king of Israel and a lovely country girl whom he met in his vineyards. This is not a fantasy storybook. It presents true-to-life episodes dealing with real-life situations so that, 3000 years later, we may read it and know that this marriage truly pleased and honored God. If you're a first-time reader, you may be surprised to find such expressions of love in the Bible.

Song of Songs illustrates the need for emotional, spiritual, and physical give-and-take for rich and meaningful sexual intimacy. Men and women are uniquely different in the way they respond sexually, so you must explore the mysterious and unusual ways of pleasing your wife. Remember that women respond to sex more in terms of caring, sharing, hugging, and kissing than we do. Slow down and enjoy that side of intimacy.

Today's Action

- ◆ Kiss your wife and tell her you love her. Ask what you can do to make your intimacy more pleasurable.

Prayer

Father God, teach me through Scripture how to be a loving husband who doesn't rush ahead of my wife. Amen.

A Spirit of Love

Let your speech always be with grace, seasoned,
as it were, with salt, so that you may know how
you should respond to each person.

—Colossians 4:6

----◇----

Have you witnessed a well-meaning Christian sharing the gospel to a possible convert—but cringed at his style? Perhaps his words were arrogant, loud, cocky, and certainly not filled with love. I wince when I witness such an abuse to our style and manner of life. Scripture says that our speech is to be filled with grace, and we are to respond properly in all occasions. I heard an amusing story that illustrates this point.

> A sophomore had backed a meek little freshman into a corner and was bombarding him with an impressive string of scientific facts. He said, "Did you know that...? Are you aware of...? Does it interest you...?"
>
> Finally, the beleaguered freshman got a word in edgewise. "Well, there is one thing you don't know," he said, half-crying.
>
> The sophomore snapped back, "And just what is that?"
>
> "You don't know," sobbed the freshman, "that you are standing on my sore foot."

People will turn away from the gospel if we are insensitive and harsh. In *Lifestyle Evangelism*, Dr. Joe Aldrich points out that we are to meet people where their needs are so they will hear what we have to say. Jesus sends us to *heal* the brokenhearted.

Today's Action

◆ Make sure that you aren't standing on someone's sore foot.

Prayer

Father God, give me a spirit of encouragement and gentleness. Amen.

The Simple Life

The fruit of the Spirit is love, joy, peace, patience, kindness, goodness, faithfulness, gentleness, self-control; against such things there is no law.

—Galatians 5:22,23

Not too long ago an extensive survey was conducted in the United States by a leading polling agency. Questionnaires were distributed to people of various ages and occupations. The key question was: What are you looking for most in life? When the results were compiled, the analysts were surprised. Most of them had expected answers that would suggest materialistic goals, but the top three things that people wanted in life were love, joy, and peace—the first three fruits of the Spirit!

Often we look around and think that the world might offer greater satisfaction in life, but that's not true. We of kindred spirit have what the world is seeking in the wrong places (usually).

The Christian life satisfies the deepest and most vital needs of the human heart. Emilie and I are acquainted with a very fine couple who have everything in material things. They have diligently worked and saved to have the best. However, recently the wife told her husband that she wanted a divorce. Her chief complaint was that she wanted to live a simpler life: not as much to polish and clean; not as many cars to drive; not as much home to take care of. In her own way she wanted love, joy, and peace.

Today's Action
- ◆ Seek to exhibit love, joy, and peace today.

Prayer
Father God, teach me how to develop and share the fruits of Your love. Amen.

Making Time for God

I shall call upon [the Lord] as long as I live.

—Psalm 116:2b

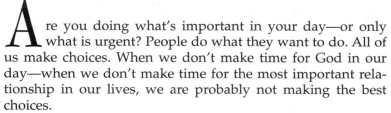

Are you doing what's important in your day—or only what is urgent? People do what they want to do. All of us make choices. When we don't make time for God in our day—when we don't make time for the most important relationship in our lives, we are probably not making the best choices.

God greatly desires to spend time alone with you. After all, you are His child (see John 1:12; Galatians 3:26). He created you, He loves you, and He gave His only Son for your salvation.

So make it a priority to spend time with God daily. There isn't a single right time or one correct place—your meeting time with God will vary according to the season of your life and the schedules you are juggling. Capture that little wasted moment when you are waiting in line, waiting for an appointment, waiting on someone, or waiting at a stoplight. Times and places where you meet God may change, but the fact that you meet alone with Him each day should be a constant in your life.

What should you do in your time alone with God? You can read and meditate on God's Word. You can spend some time in prayer. Talk to Him as you would to your earthly parents or a special friend who loves you.

Remember, too, that you can talk to Him anytime. You don't have to make an appointment to ask Him for something you need or to thank Him for something you have received.

He always loves to hear from you. God is interested in everything that happens to you.

Today's Action

- ◆ If you are not already spending time with God each day, decide to give it a try for one month. Then set aside a time, and stick to it.

Prayer

Father God, thank You for being within the sound of my voice and only a thought distance away. Amen.

The War Against Values

All things are lawful for me, but not all things are profitable.

—1 Corinthians 6:12

———◇———

No greater influence impacts our thinking more than the media. Unfortunately, the media in America is controlled by secular humanists so the slant of most print copy, programming, advertising, and news portrays a secular life view.

Secular humanism is the view that man establishes his own moral values apart from the influence of anyone (including God), and he self-determines his own destiny. He is the "master of his own fate."

The problem with such a life view is that it has no absolutes. Everything is relative; there is no eternal reference point. People can make up their own rules as they go. How do we know if sexual promiscuity is immoral or not? Why shouldn't we cheat in business? Why should family life be considered more important than a career?

Ted Koppel, the news anchor for ABC's "Nightline," in a commencement address at Duke University said: "We have reconstructed the tower of Babel and it is a television antenna, a thousand voices producing a daily parody of democracy in which everyone's opinion is afforded equal weight regardless of substance or merit. This means we need to guard our minds more carefully because so many kooky ideas are floating around."

Perhaps the only way to overcome this impact is to reevaluate our sources of entertainment and information. We should be concerned that our subconscious minds might be swayed in an area in which we have difficulty resisting. Our subconscious mind has no walls around it and no sentinel at the gate.

Today's Action

◆ Think about the role that TV plays in your home. If nerves are on edge, tempers are flaring, and people are angry, these could be signs of dependence on television for entertainment and escape. As a father, take the lead in getting this "stealer of time" under control. Be selective in what comes in and when. Turn off TV during times when the family comes together for meals, discussions, activities, devotions, and homework.

Prayer

Father God, make me and my family aware of those things that steal from us. Give us the courage to be strong. Amen.

Family life is full of major and minor crises—the ups and downs of health, success and failure in career, marriage, and divorce—and all kinds of characters. It is tied to places and events and histories. With all of these felt details, life etches itself into memory and personality. It's difficult to imagine anything more nourishing to the soul.

—*Thomas Moore*

A Balanced Home

Unless the LORD builds the house, they labor in vain who build it; unless the LORD guards the city, the watchman keeps awake in vain.

—Psalm 127:1

---◇---

As parents we sometimes wonder if we actually have a home—or is it merely a stopover place to eat, do laundry, hang around, and sleep? Is it just a place to repair things, mow the lawn, paint, wallpaper, and install new carpet? A true home is much more than all that. It is a place of people living, growing, laughing, crying, learning, and creating together.

A small child, after watching his house burn down, was quoted as saying, "We still have a home. We just don't have a house to put it in." How perceptive!

Our home should be a trauma center for the whole family. We don't have to be perfect—just forgiven. We can grow, we can make mistakes, we can shout for joy, we can cry, we can agree, and we can disagree. Home is a place where happy experiences occur. It's a place sheltered from the problems of the world, a place of love, acceptance, and security.

When we read the newspaper we are confronted with all the tragedies around us, and we realize that the world outside our front door is falling apart. But within our four walls we can offer a place of peace.

What can we do to have a home like God intended? As with everything in life, when something is broken we go back to the instruction book—and life's manual is the Bible. The home is God's idea. He designed the home to be the foundation of society—a place to meet the mental, spiritual, physical, and emotional needs of people.

The members of a family must work together to make their house a true home—not just a place where they live.

Solomon spoke to this subject in Proverbs 24:3,4. He outlined three basic principles of building a balanced home:

◆ wisdom
◆ understanding
◆ knowledge

It is impossible to do this by our own efforts; we aren't strong enough to accomplish the task. We must guide our hearts, souls, and lives to God's Son, Jesus Christ. He is our source of strength.

Today's Action

◆ Pray for your home and your family members.

Prayer

Father God, give my family and me wisdom, understanding, and knowledge, and help us turn our house into a home. Amen.

Show Your Love

Do you love Me more than these?

—John 21:15

❏
❏
❏

————◇————

D r. J. Hamilton gives a very vivid description of Christian love:

> When a rosebud is formed, if the soil is soft, and the sky is genial, it is not long before it bursts; for the life within is so abundant that it can no longer contain it all, but in blossomed brightness and swimming fragrance it must needs let forth its joy, and gladden all the air. And if, when thus ripe, it refused to expand, it would quickly rot at heart, and die. And Christian love is just piety with its petals fully spread, developing itself, and making it a happier world. The religion which fancies that it loves God, when it never evinces love to its brother, is not piety, but a poor mildewed theology, a dogma with a worm in the heart.

The best proof of love for God is love for one another. How are your relationships going? Are there some that need repair? If so, now is a good time to straighten out any difficulty you might have with a friend.

Our Lord also looks for an "I love You" from His children that is backed up by action. When He asked Peter, "Do you love Me?" He was not satisfied with a casual, "Sure, Lord, You know I do!" The question came again and again. Each time Jesus responded to His disciple's reply by saying in effect, "Peter, if you love Me, care for those I care for. Peter, if you love Me, follow Me." With each response Jesus was telling

Peter, "If you love Me, tend My lambs and tend My sheep." If there is love, there is a sign that reflects that love. Jesus said, in essence, if you love Me do something to show your love for Me.

What would you say if the Lord were to ask if you loved Him? Would you answer, "Yes, Lord, I love You"? Oh, may our words delight the Father's heart because they come from obedient children!

Today's Action

◆ Discover ways to show your love for Christ today, then do them.

Prayer

Jesus, give me direction to follow Your command to tend Your sheep. Amen.

A Common Commitment

*Then Isaac. . .took Rebekah, and she became his
wife; and he loved her.*

—Genesis 24:67

———————◇———————

I saac was not a dynamic man like his father Abraham. Yet
his singular love for Rebekah stands in sharp contrast to
the other patriarchs of his time, who had concubines and
many wives. Nothing in the Scriptures suggests that he ever
followed that practice. He is portrayed as a kind, loving, faithful husband.

When Emilie and I have the opportunity to meet couples
who have been married 40-plus years, we love to hear of their
courtship and marriage. All have had rocky roads along the
way, but they share a common commitment—they have stuck
it out. They all express their joy by saying, "I'm so glad we
endured the rough times, now we are truly receiving God's
blessing for being obedient."

Old-fashioned life-time commitments. Many people are
glad for easy divorce laws that make possible quick releases
from uncomfortableness when their marriages enter trouble-
some times. But true love endures in spite of difficulties. Paul
says "love never fails" (1 Corinthians 13:8).

It does not depend upon the continuance of pleasing qualities in the loved one. The best couples have times that aren't
always pleasing. Create a deep desire in your heart and soul to
look after the welfare of your mate. Let it grow more enduring
the older you become.

Today's Action

- ◆ Do something today that shows your mate how important her welfare is to you.

Prayer

*Father God, thank You for giving me my wife. Help me love and
care for her. Amen.*

Serving with Humility

Have this attitude in yourselves which was also in Christ Jesus.

—Philippians 2:5

———————◇———————

E ach time I blow it this verse crosses my mind and leads me to a self-talk that goes like this: "Thank You, Lord, for revealing to me that I've still got a long way to go before I have your attitude—one of humility." Yes, the Lord continually gives me the opportunity to realize that I need to work on developing humbleness.

Since the media constantly bombard us with the importance of self-esteem, it's easy to become confused about what genuine humility is. Having the mind and heart and attitude of Christ is a good start. Philippians 2:3 says, "Do nothing out of selfish ambition or vain conceit, but in humility consider others better than yourself" (NIV).

It is out of strength, not weakness, that we grow in humility. Dr. Bruce Narramore says that humility has three elements:

- ◆ recognition that you need God.
- ◆ a realistic evaluation of your abilities.
- ◆ a willingness to serve.

As we serve others, we need to do it with a right heart—seeking to please God, not desiring any glory or honor for ourselves.

Today's Action
- ◆ In what three capacities or organizations would you be willing to serve? This week, step forward and volunteer your services in one of these areas.

Prayer
Father God, I need to learn to give myself away to others. Teach me humility. Amen.

Every Child Is Unique

*Train up a child in the way he should go, even
when he is old he will not depart from it.*

—Proverbs 22:6

———————◇———————

As I look at our five grandchildren—Christine, Chad,
Bevan, Bradley Joe, and Weston—I find myself face-to-
face with the challenge of understanding each of them so that
I can help them develop godly characters. I realize that each of
them is a unique individual with different perspectives.

In raising our own children, Brad and Jennifer, Emilie and
I realized that we had to teach, motivate, and discipline each
of them according to his or her unique personality. God helped
us understand that children need to be trained in a way tailor-
made for them. In today's verse, Solomon's idea communi-
cates that we parents are to continue training our children as
long as they are under our care, and we are to train our children
God's way—not according to our ideas, our ways, or our plans.

It's important to see that this verse is not a guarantee to
parents that raising children God's way means they will never
stray from His path. But our efforts to train our children to follow God will be most effective when we use the methods most
appropriate to their individual personalities. We need to
approach each child differently and not compare them to each
other. We need to be a student of our children. This gives our
children a solid, biblical foundation for their lives.

Today's Action
- ◆ Learn one new thing about each of your children today—
  then do something positive with that information.

Prayer
*Father God, please give me insight into each of my children.
Help me understand who they are and the best way to reach them.
Amen.*

Parents have become so convinced that educators know what is best for their children that they forget that they themselves are really the experts.

—*Marian Wright Edelman*

Drink Deeply Today

If any man is thirsty, let him come to Me and drink.

—John 7:37

❏
❏
❏

————————◇————————

A little girl from a very poor family was in the hospital. The nurse brought her a glass filled to the brim with milk. This was the first time the girl had a whole glass of her own since she usually had to share with her brothers and sisters. When the nurse returned to her room, she found the glass still full.

"Why didn't you drink it?" she asked.

"You didn't tell me how deep I could drink."

The nurse fought back tears. "Drink all of it," she said tenderly. "This whole glass is just for you."

The latest health information on drinking water is that we should drink before we get thirsty. If we wait until we feel thirsty, then we've already started to dehydrate. That's the way it is with God. In our timidity we have a tendency to take just a small sip, but Jesus tells us to drink. Don't wait until a problem arises before you develop a prayer life. Pray during good times so that you know how to pray in the hard times.

The moment a spiritual need arises, invite God to fill it: When on the verge of losing your temper, pray, "Thy patience, Lord." When alone, "Thy presence, Lord." When anxious, "Thy peace, Lord." When tempted by lustful thoughts, "Thy purity, Lord."

Today's Action

◆ Come to Jesus and gulp freely of his everlasting water.

Prayer

Father God, thank You for letting me drink freely from your cup of life. Amen.

Overcoming Rejection

For God so loved the world, that He gave His only begotten Son.

—John 3:16

❏
❏
❏

———◇———

Nothing hurts a male ego as much as rejection. When have you experienced that in your life? Did it come from a special girl in high school, a failed college exam, a missed promotion, a home loan that wasn't approved? How did you react to this rejection? Were you hurt? Angry? Whom did you go to?

You and I can go to Jesus when we're rebuffed. He who was nailed to the cross knows about rejection. Jesus shouted to God in heaven, "My God, my God, why have you forsaken me?" (Matthew 27:46 NIV). Despite all of Jesus' rejections, He never abandoned the mission God had given Him, never retaliated against those who scorned Him, and responded in love to those who tried to offend Him.

Jesus gives us His grace to help us when we're hurting. These promises are for us:

- "Never will I leave you" (Hebrews 13:5 NIV)
- "Praise be to God . . . who comforts us in all our troubles" (2 Corinthians 1:3,4).
- "You were marked in him with a seal" (Ephesians 1:13)

Today's Action

- Make a list of the times you've experienced rejection. What has God taught you through these events?

Prayer

Father God, help me use these rejections to become more like You. Amen.

Fear or Love?

Everyone who has left houses or brothers or sisters or father or mother or children or farms for My name's sake, shall receive many times as much.

—Matthew 19:29

———◇———

Why do we do what we do? Through the years I've asked myself again and again, "Why do I serve? What is my motivation for speaking, writing, giving to the church, being a father, a grandfather, and loving my wife and family?" To put it more bluntly, What will I get as a result of my efforts?

Peter asked Jesus, "We have left everything and followed You; what then will there be for us?"

Jesus answered Peter's question and said to him—and us—what benefits we get when we serve God and His kingdom:

- We will receive a hundred times as much as we give up (NIV).
- We will inherit eternal life.
- Many who are first will be last, and many who are last will be first.

These rewards are gracious and generous, but are you letting them motivate your service to God? Or do you, like many people, think God will punish you if you don't serve Him.

My own list of blessings continues on and on, each item reminding me that God does indeed take care of His people when they sacrifice to serve Him.

Today's Action

- List at least ten of your blessings. What does this list show you about God?

Prayer

Father God, show me my true motivation for serving You. Amen.

118

Finding Right Priorities

Let each of us please his neighbor for his good, to his edification.

—Romans 15:2

———◇———

I n one of his books, Leslie B. Flynn has a chapter entitled, "You Aim to Please—But Whom?" He points out that many Christians refuse to take responsibilities in the church because they are living only to please themselves. They enjoy weekend travel, so they don't want to commit to picking up children for Sunday school, teaching a class, or assuming other duties that require regular attendance. They put their own interests ahead of the work of the Lord.

Time is so precious that families cry out for the weekend so they can really start living.

In many homes both parents work full-time and the weekend is the only time to do the chores. The children are excited because mom and dad are home so now they can go to the ball game, a picnic, a sleep-over with a friend, and on and on.

Soon we find we have shoved God into a corner of our lives to gather dust. All the weekend activities can rob us of what's important in life. As dads we must yell "stop" and get together with mom to discuss what's important in life.

Your children's formative years are so important. Golf can wait; it will be there long after your children are grown and out of the nest. Yes, we all try to please someone, but whom? That's the basic question we all wrestle with.

Today's Action

◆ Volunteer to teach Sunday school at church.

Prayer

Father God, help me think beyond myself and share with others what You have given to me. Amen.

The Command to Love

You shall love the LORD your God with all your heart and with all your soul and with all your might.

—Deuteronomy 6:5

———◇———

Jesus Christ called this the first and greatest commandment (see Mark 12:30). Today's verse, along with Matthew 22:36-38 talks about three basic loves—love of God, love of neighbor, and love of self. What a difference we would make in the world if we were able to love in these ways! Clearly, the command to love is important to God. But as we try to remain constantly aware of God's command, how do we live out these loves? In Ephesians 5:19-21 we get a small glimpse on how to love this way. If we—

- ◆ love ourselves we will speak and sing words of joy. We will make music in our hearts for the Lord.

- ◆ love God we will always give thanks for all things in the name of our Lord Jesus Christ. Positive words will flow from our lips unto God.

- ◆ love our neighbors we will be subject one to another in fear of Christ. We will be willing to allow another person's needs to take precedence over our own. This submission is to be based on our reverence for God. We can't do it on our human power.

These are great actions for our Christian growth, but we must start by loving God with all our hearts, souls, strength, and minds—then we can move out to share with others.

Today's Action
- ◆ Write down several ways you can love God.

Prayer
Father God, help us to better understand what kind of love You want us to have. Amen.

Only when you're studying and applying God's truth in the Bible can you discern what's right or wrong, true or false, loving or cruel, profitable or foolish, noble or cowardly.

Known by Jesus

*I am the good shepherd; and I know My own,
and My own know me.*

—John 10:14

———————◇———————

Have you ever had that sick feeling when someone didn't notice you? You felt rejected and of little worth. You were lost in the crowd. You thought, *Who cares about little old me?* In the midst of this computer age, it seems like we have just become a number. Even our junk mail is addressed to "resident." We receive form letters back from an inquiry or an e-mail reply rather than a thank-you note.

When Edward VII, the king of England from 1901 to 1910, was visiting a city to lay the cornerstone for a new hospital, thousands of schoolchildren were present to sing for him. Following the ceremony, the King walked past the excited youngsters. After he was gone, a teacher saw one of her students crying. She asked her, "Why are you crying? Did you not see the king?" "Yes," the young girl sobbed, "but the king did not see me."

There was no way that King Edward should have been expected to notice every individual in that throng of people. Jesus, however, does give personal attention to each one of us. Jesus calls His own sheep by name. How does He do that? I'm not sure, but from experience I know He cares for me. I can hear His voice in Scripture and in song. What an awesome thought to think that Jesus knows who we are. We matter to Him. How can we have a poor image of ourselves when we are known by God? We are important to the creator of the universe.

Today's Action

- ◆ Act with assurance that you are known by God. Tell someone else about that knowledge and experience.

Prayer

Father God, thank You for making me more than my Social Security number. Thank You for knowing me. Amen.

Submission

Be subject to one another in the fear of Christ.

—Ephesians 5:21

❑
❑
❑

———◇———

E milie, I'm going out to run a few errands, would you like me to stop off at the market and pick-up anything for dinner?"

"Bob, is there anything special you would like for dinner?"

"Christine, how are you doing with school supplies? I'll be out and about, can I pick you up anything you might need?"

"Ken, I hear your family is sick with colds, do they need any medicine that I might bring over?"

What do these questions exhibit? That someone is concerned about someone else and willing to serve.

Ephesians 5:21 is one of Emilie's and my favorite verses. We want to be subject one to another out of respect for our Lord. If we men step out and begin to serve our family members we won't have to demand respect. It will be there on everyone's lips. When we have established a record of servanthood, all other areas of leadership will fall into place.

Wives don't object to being under the authority of their husbands—when the husbands have been serving them and their children. The wives can trust them to be concerned about their needs. Husbands are to love their wives as Christ loves the church (see Ephesians 5:25).

Today's Action

◆ Do something today for your wife that shows you love and respect her.

Prayer

Father God, thank You for showing me how to love successfully in marriage. Amen.

Creating a Master Plan

And the man said, "This is now bone of my
bones, and flesh of my flesh; she shall be called
Woman, because she was taken out of Man."

—Genesis 2:23

———————◇———————

In his best-selling book *Talking Straight*, Lee Iacocca talks about the importance of family.

> My father told me that the best way to teach is by example. He certainly showed me what it took to be a good person and a good citizen. No one ever said on his deathbed, "I should have spent more time on my business." Throughout my life I've worried most that my children would turn out right.

> The only rock I know that stays steady, the only institution I know that works, is the family. I was brought up to believe in it and I do. You can't have a country, city, or a state that's worth anything unless you govern within yourself in your day-to-day life. It all starts at home.

Our reading for today reminds us that God established the family. Although modern life is trying its hardest to minimize the family as an institution, we know that whatever God begins He will not abandon.

Have you and your mate taken time to draft a master plan for your family? What it should look like—its values, guidelines, dreams, and aspirations? In order for our society to survive, we must have strong, healthy families.

Today's Action

- ◆ Write your plans down and include specific goals for your family's life.

Prayer

Father God, create in me a hunger to search out Your plan for my life and my family. Amen.

God Continually Provides

Do not be afraid, for am I in God's place? You
meant evil against me but God meant it for good
in order to bring about this present result.

—Genesis 50:20,21

———◇———

The story of Joseph and his family, which begins in Genesis 37, is a terrific example of how God provides for us. In brief summary:

> Jacob favored his son Joseph. Extremely jealous, his brothers plotted against Joseph and sold him as a slave. But God was with Joseph. He ended up in Egypt, where he was a trusted servant of Pharaoh. Now Joseph was the grain overseer, so when Jacob sent his sons to Egypt to buy grain they encountered Joseph, but didn't recognize him.

Genesis 50:19,20 shares Joseph's words as he revealed himself to his brothers. The wisdom that "God causes all things to work together for the good to those who love God" (Romans 8:28), can be stated—

> All the events of life are precious to one that has this simple connection with Christ of faith and love. No wind can blow wrong, no event be mistimed, no result disastrous. If God but cares for our inward and external life, if, by all the experiences of this life, he is reducing it, and preparing for its disclosure, nothing can befall us but prosperity. Every sorrow shall be but the setting of some luminous jewel of joy. Our every morning shall be but the enamel around the diamond; our very hardships but the metallic rim that hold the opal, glancing with strange interior fires.

> —Buches

Yes, we can trust God that even the evildoers play a part in developing us into what God wants us to become. Trust Him for every event in your life.

Today's Action

◆ Is God changing any bad situations in your life to work for your good? List them.

Prayer

Father God, let me trust You more in all the circumstances of my life. Amen.

Jesus Weeps with You

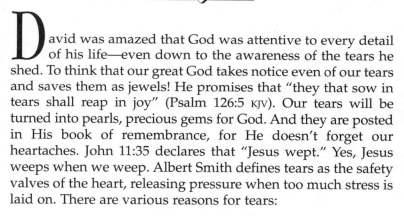

Thou hast taken account of my wanderings; put my tears in Thy bottle; are they not in Thy book?

—Psalm 56:8

D avid was amazed that God was attentive to every detail of his life—even down to the awareness of the tears he shed. To think that our great God takes notice even of our tears and saves them as jewels! He promises that "they that sow in tears shall reap in joy" (Psalm 126:5 KJV). Our tears will be turned into pearls, precious gems for God. And they are posted in His book of remembrance, for He doesn't forget our heartaches. John 11:35 declares that "Jesus wept." Yes, Jesus weeps when we weep. Albert Smith defines tears as the safety valves of the heart, releasing pressure when too much stress is laid on. There are various reasons for tears:

- ◆ tears of love which burst from our hearts
- ◆ tears of sorrow as a mother weeps for her wayward son
- ◆ tears of joy
- ◆ tears of exhortation and forgiveness
- ◆ tears of compassion
- ◆ tears of spiritual desire and hope

Today's Action
- ◆ Don't be afraid to shed tears when they swell up from your heart. Be willing to release them.

Prayer
Father God, let me be open enough with my wife and family that I can show my emotions—even my tears. Amen.

Daily Blessing and Grace

Incorporating the principle of Ephesians 5:21, we are to be submissive to one another. Run an errand, do something for your mate without being asked, give small gifts, give a compliment when appropriate, be willing to say "I'm sorry."

A Kindred Spirit

There is a friend who sticks closer than a brother.

—Proverbs 18:24

❑
❑
❑

———◇———

A mouse one day happened to run across the paws of a sleeping lion and awakened him. The lion, angry at being disturbed, grabbed the mouse and was about to swallow him when the mouse cried out, "Please, kind sir, I didn't mean it. If you will let me go, I shall always be grateful, and perhaps I can help you someday."

The idea that such a little thing as a mouse could help him so amused the lion that he let the mouse go. A week later the mouse heard a lion roaring loudly. He went closer to see what the trouble was and found his lion caught in a hunter's net. Remembering his promise, the mouse began to gnaw the ropes of the net and kept it up until the lion could get free. The lion then acknowledged that little friends might prove great friends.

—An Aesop fable

Friends and friendships are unique social happenings. Often I wonder why some people are attracted to others. Is it because of common interests, past experiences, physical attractions, having children that are friends with another family's kids, or attending the same church? What is it that bonds people together?

As I consider the many friends I have, I sense it's a little of all of the above. My friends come from various backgrounds, religions, economic levels, and educational achievement.

There does, however, seem to be one common strand that runs through most of these friendships. We have a kindred spirit in the Lord.

The writer of today's proverb gives a warning in the first part of verse 24: "A man of many friends comes to ruin." When I first read that I was confused. I thought to myself, "I thought we were to have a lot of friends, so why this warning?" But as I thought about it, a thought came to me. He was stressing that too many friends chosen indiscriminately will bring trouble, but a genuine friend sticks with you through thick and thin. When we use this criterion for a friend, we begin to thin the acquaintance ranks down to those who are truly our friends.

I know without a doubt that several of my friends would be with me no matter what the circumstances, what day of the week, and what time of the day or night I needed help. I call these my "two A.M. friends."

As in the Aesop story, you never know when you will need a friend. I have found that those who have friends are themselves friendly. They go out of their way to be a friend. In order to have friends, one must be a friend.

Friendship-making is a skill we need to teach our children. As parents, we have only a short window of opportunity to teach the value of positive friendships. Each year we have less influence on them because the music, dress, dance, and jewelry selections of the world seem to pull our children from our group. While there is still time, we need to teach our youngsters how to choose the right kind of friends.

Today's Action

- ◆ Write a friend a note expressing how much you appreciate his or her friendship.

Prayer

Father God, You have given me some wonderful friends. I thank You for who they are to me. Amen.

Final Quake

In various places there will be famines and earthquakes.

—Matthew 24:7

———◇———

On January 17, 1994, at 4:31 A.M. the Los Angeles area was rocked by an earthquake ranked 6.6 on the Richter scale. Living one hour east of the epicenter, we felt the strength of the quake. This quake shook up and down, not the rolling motions we've felt in the past. Almost all of Southern California awoke out of a dead sleep. Many ran into the streets or crawled under beds, desks, tables, and doorways. Our phone rang. It was our son Brad. "Dad, this was a bad one. Los Angeles has been hit hard," he said. He was correct. Fatalities mounted and damages rose to billions of dollars. Freeways fell, fires broke out, and the devastation was massive.

Only three months earlier, Southern California had been hit by major fires, then rain caused mud slides in multimillion-dollar home areas. In that short time we experienced most of what the Scripture talks about—riots, earthquakes, fires, and flooding. There's also drive-by shootings, gangs, car-jackings, murders, and thefts of all kinds. The safety factor in this part of the country has dropped dramatically.

Yet why are we surprised? Our text tells us that before the Lord returns these things will happen. We must be ready. California residents keep bottled water, earthquake kits, and installed gas shut-off valves in an attempt to prepare for the "big one." Well, January 17 was almost it. The cleanup and rebuilding took years. But time passed, people forgot, and we proceeded on with the fast pace of L.A. life.

We must be ready in an eternal way. We need to prepare ourselves spiritually for the future "quake" of Jesus' return.

He is coming again and, just as the earth trembles at unexpected times, we won't know the time, day, or place of His arrival. Our Lord will come when we least expect Him.

I tell you from experience that when the earth quakes fear flies through your body. But that sensation will not even be close to the heated fear and trembling of those who are not ready when the Lord returns. Jesus says in John 11:25,26, "I am the resurrection and the life; he who believes in Me shall live even if he dies. And whoever lives and believes in Me shall never die...." This is what we must believe to be ready. So simple, yet so many reject it.

Remember, the Bible is truth. When the last call comes, be ready to meet your Lord and Savior.

Believing is receiving.

Today's Action

- ◆ Write in your journal or in your Bible the date and time you invited Jesus to be your Savior.

Prayer

Father God, may Your spirit speak to those who do not know You as their Savior. Amen.

Boldly Say No

*Rest in the LORD and wait patiently for Him; do
not fret because of him who prospers in his way.*

—Psalm 37:7a

Steven R. Covey, in his book, *The Seven Habits of Highly Effective People*, tells a story that reflects the need for renewal and reawakening in our lives.

> Suppose you came upon a man in the woods feverishly sawing down a tree.
>
> "You look exhausted!" you exclaim. "How long have you been at it?"
>
> "Over five hours," he replies, "and I'm beat. This is hard."
>
> "Maybe you could take a break for a few minutes and sharpen that saw. Then the work would go faster."
>
> "No time," the man says emphatically. "I'm too busy sawing."

To sharpen the saw means renewing ourselves in all four aspects of our natures:

> *Physical*—exercise, nutrition, stress management;
> *Mental*—reading, thinking, planning, writing;
> *Social/Emotional*—service, empathy, security;
> *Spiritual*—spiritual reading, study, and meditation.

To exercise in all these necessary dimensions, we must be proactive. No one can do it for us or make it urgent for us. We must do it for ourselves.

If we are to stay on top of the pile rather than under the pile, we must take time to sharpen the saws of our lives. Since I speak to various groups, I find many men who are defeated and burned out from their roles in life. Many express to me, "If I only had time for myself, I would stop and smell the roses!"

I find that if I look back over my shoulder there is a competitor there ready to pass me. It seems like there is no letting up. Everyone wants it faster and faster—hurry, hurry. We've got to come to grips with our lives and take control. There are times when we have to boldly say, "No!"

Today's Action

◆ Stop sawing and get your saw sharpened.

Prayer

Father God, oh, how I need to learn to wait upon You. Give me courage to say "No!" Amen.

The Truth About Wisdom

The fear of the Lord *is the beginning of knowl-*
edge; fools despise wisdom and instruction.

—Proverbs 1:7

❑
❑
❑

—————◇—————

R obert Fulghum, in his book *All I Really Need To Know I
Learned in Kindergarten,* gives us an introduction of learning about the important concepts of life. He writes,

> Most of what I really need to know about how to
> live, and what to do, and how to be, I learned in
> kindergarten. Wisdom was not at the top of the
> graduate school mountain but there in the sandbox
> at nursery school.

> These are things I learned: Share everything. Play
> fair. Don't hit people. Put things back where you
> found them. Clean up your own mess. Don't take
> things that aren't yours. Say you're sorry when you
> hurt someone. Wash your hands before you eat.
> Flush. Warm cookies and cold milk are good for
> you. Live a balanced life. Learn some and think
> some and draw and paint and sing and dance and
> play and work some every day.

> Take a nap every afternoon. When you go out into
> the world, watch for traffic, hold hands, and stick
> together. Be aware of wonder. Remember the little
> seed in the plastic cup. The roots go down and the
> plant goes up and nobody really knows how or
> why, but we are all like that.

> Goldfish and hamsters and white mice and even the
> little seed in the plastic cup—they all die. So do we.

And then remember the book about Dick and Jane and the first word you learned, the biggest word of all: LOOK. Everything you need to know is in there somewhere. The Golden Rule and love and basic sanitation. Ecology and politics and sane living.

Think of what a better world it would be if we all—the whole world—had cookies and milk about 3 o'clock every afternoon and then lay down with our blankets for a nap. Or if we had a basic policy in our nation and other nations to always put things back where we found them and cleaned up our own messes. And it is still true, no matter how old you are, when you go out into the world it is best to hold hands and stick together.

The knowledge that Solomon's wise sayings offer us goes beyond accomplishments. His advice centers on moral responsibility—to conduct ourselves in various situations in everyday life. His fundamental instruction is to fear and trust the Lord. Solomon challenges us to continually seek God's wisdom in the decisions we make each day.

We must think clearly and scripturally if we are to survive the present culture war in America. We can't be swayed by what the secular world says.

Today's Action
- Get in the habit of answering basic questions from a theological framework.

Prayer
Father God, I want to be a man who seeks after Your knowledge. Show me Your ways. Amen.

The Perfect Manual

*But where can wisdom by found? And where is
the place of understanding?*

—Job 28:12

❑
❑
❑

———◇———

Not long ago my friend Florence Littauer wrote a book titled *Looking for Love in All the Wrong Places*. We are living in a culture that has a difficult time reading the instruction manual. For some reason we want to invent the wheel by ourselves; we have trouble seeking the truth from the wise. We look for love in all the wrong places, and we also seek wisdom in places where there is no wisdom. We talk to friends, read magazines, listen to talk shows, and attend seminars—all the wrong places to find the truth.

The writer of the book of Job struggled with this same question of life. In Job 28:12 he asked, "Where can wisdom be found?" All through chapter 28 he searched for the answer.

- ◆ Man doesn't know its value (verse 13).
- ◆ It is not found in the land of the living (verse 13).
- ◆ The inner earth says, "It's not in me" (verse 14).
- ◆ The sea says, "It's not in me" (verse 14).
- ◆ You can't buy it with gold or silver (verse 15).
- ◆ Precious stones don't have it (verse 16).
- ◆ It can't be equated with gold (verse 17).
- ◆ Pearls don't have it (verse 18).
- ◆ It is hidden from the eyes of all living creatures (verse 21).
- ◆ Birds of the sky don't have it (verse 21).
- ◆ Destruction and death say, "We have heard about it with our ears" (verse 22).
- ◆ God understands its way, and He knows its place (verse 23).

137

- ◆ God looks to the ends of the earth and sees everything under heaven (verse 24).
- ◆ God saw wisdom and declared it (verse 27).
- ◆ God established it and searched it out (verse 27).

In verse 28 God told man, "Behold, the fear of the Lord, that is wisdom." In other words, showing holy respect and reverence for God and shunning evil is wisdom.

Job and his friends claimed wisdom of themselves, but wisdom is clearly an outgrowth of God and not merely something to be obtained. Although we can know and understand many things, we cannot attain the level of Creator—wisdom. There will always be questions that only God the Creator can answer. Solomon knew that true wisdom is not found in human understanding but is from God alone (Proverbs 1:7; 9:10).

I challenge you to learn this basic truth of Scripture. Don't look in all the wrong places for your answers in life. Start with the manual that tells you step-by-step how to live life. If you want to know God's perspective, read your Bible daily.

Today's Action

- ◆ Evaluate where you are looking for wisdom. Is it in the right places?

Prayer

Father God, please close the doors to the wrong places in which I'm searching. Amen.

Compassion

Look out for the interests of others. You can't solve all the world's problems, but you can—and are called upon to—help those whom God has placed in your life.

A Special Friendship

Make my joy complete by being of the same mind, maintaining the same love, united in spirit, intent on one purpose.

—Philippians 2:2

———◇———

Paul writes of the discord within the church. It's kind of like Clint Eastwood when he uttered his famous line, "Go ahead. Make my day." Paul says, "Make my joy complete" by getting along with each other. Let's stop bickering and backbiting. Let's start getting along with each other.

Friendship is the launching pad for every love. It spills into the other important relationships of life. Friendship is the beginning of all levels of intimacy—with our mate, with our parents, with our children—with everyone we encounter. Philippians 2:2 is telling us to heal our relationships and start getting along together.

Few of us are privileged to be able to sit down and share our innermost thoughts with someone. Did you know that some research indicates that friendly people live longer than the general population?

"But how do I develop friends?" you ask. Try these basic principles:

- ◆ Make friendship a top priority.
- ◆ Be willing to take a risk and be transparent.
- ◆ Talk about your care for each other.
- ◆ Learn and exhibit the language of love and friendship.
- ◆ Give your friends room to be themselves.

Today's Action

- ◆ Do something for your wife that lets her know she is your friend.

Prayer

Father God, I truly want to make my mate my special friend. Help me have a new beginning today. Amen.

A Rich and Creamy Life

I will meditate on Thy precepts, and regard Thy ways.

—Psalm 119:15

❑
❑
❑

---◇---

Wherever Emilie and I travel, we find the same fast-food restaurants. We have become a nation of fast-food junkies. In Southern California one of the major fast-food chains has just introduced a new 200-million-dollar ad campaign directed toward men, because research shows that more men eat in fast-food establishments than women. As a nation, we're constantly on the go, and sometimes even fast-food places seem slow!

Contrast this idea of constantly hurrying with the idea given in today's verse. It says we are to meditate on God's precepts. When we *meditate* that's slow. Sort of like a cow chewing her cud. Why do cows spend so much time chewing their cud? Cows first fill their stomachs with grass and other food. Then they begin the long chew. They bring the food back up from their stomachs and chew and chew what they've already swallowed. This process transforms the food into rich creamy milk. Time consuming? Yes. But it's a must if you want good milk. That's the way it is with us as Christians. If we want to grow, we must slow down and meditate on God's principles. We need to read God's Word then study its meaning.

Today's Action
♦ Slow down and chew the cud of God's Word.

Prayer
Father God, let me take joy in meditating upon Your words. I want to become a mature Christian. Amen.

Impractical Idealism?

> *Blessed are those who hunger and thirst for righteousness for they shall be satisfied.*
>
> **—Matthew 5:6**

———◇———

Columnist Sidney J. Harris wrote about the negative effects of impractical idealism. He described an author who had so much to give in his books, but so little to offer in real life. When Harris first read this writer's works, he thought they were "like a breath of fresh air in a fetid chamber. . . . He was big on Humanity, with a capital H, on family ties and folkways and children and animals and flowers." But, as Harris laments, it was not an idealism borne out in the author's life. At home the man was a tyrant and a terror. He had an unrealistic ideal of what others should be.

We struggle every day to keep a proper balance between what is ideal and what is real. We talk the good walk, but somehow we have difficulty putting it into practice. We desperately want to do what delights each of our hearts, but we fall short in implementation.

In the Sermon on the Mount (Matthew 5–7), the Lord Jesus teaches us to combine idealism with realism. He shows us how to have the proper balance so we don't get so wrapped up in the everyday circumstances of life that we lose vision of what life can be.

If we follow Jesus' examples, we will hold on to His values and desires for our lives as well as keep in touch with the real world. Read the Scriptures to make sure your Christian walk is as fulfilling as possible.

Today's Action

* ◆ Hunger and thirst after righteousness.

Prayer

Father God, fill my heart with Your goodness and righteousness. Amen.

Who Moved Away?

Behold, like the clay in the potter's hand, so are
you in My hand.

—Jeremiah 18:6

———————◇———————

When our son, Brad, was in elementary school, the teacher asked the class to shape clay into something. Molded and shaped with his small hands, this red dinosaur-type thing that Brad proudly brought home is still on our bookshelf today.

Later, in high school, Brad enrolled in a ceramics class. His first pieces were crooked and misshapen, but as time went on he made some pieces of real art—vases, pots, pitchers, and various other kinds of pottery. Many pieces of clay he threw on the pottery wheel, however, took a different direction than he'd intended. Brad would work and work to reshape the clay, and sometimes he would have to start all over, working and working to make it exactly the way he wanted it to be.

With each one of us, God has, so to speak, taken a handful of clay to make us exactly who He wants us to be. He is the Master Potter, and we are the vessels in His hands. As He shapes us on the potter's wheel, He works on the inside and the outside. He says, "I am with you. I am the Lord of your life and I will build within you a strong foundation based upon My Word."

The Master Potter also uses the circumstances of life to shape us. But when a child dies, we lose our jobs, fire destroys our homes, finances dissolve, our marriages fall apart, or our children rebel, the Potter can seem very far away. We may feel forgotten by God so we pull away from Him because He "let us down." As time passes, God seems even more distant, and it seems like the Potter's work is put on hold. But God said, "I will not fail you or forsake you" (Joshua 1:5).

When we feel far from God, we need to remember that He didn't put us on the shelf. We are the ones who moved away. He's ready to continue molding us into the people He intends us to be.

In pottery, the clay is baked at a very high temperature to set the clay so the vessel won't leak. Sometimes the true beauty of the clay comes out only after the firing. The fires of life can do the same for our faith and our character. When we go through trials we can rest in the knowledge that the Master Potter is at work.

Today's Action

- ◆ Give back to God what you have taken away from Him because you didn't feel you could trust Him: your family, your home, your weight, your looks, your salary.

Prayer

Father God, help me to trust You more each day as I give back what belongs to You. Amen.

Be Prepared When the Storm Hits

*And He shall be the stability of your times, a
wealth of salvation, wisdom, and knowledge; the
fear of the Lord is his treasure.*

—**Isaiah 33:6**

❏
❏
❏

———◇———

In this crazy world of ours, I'm always losing my foundation. I place my trust in politicians, and they fail me. I look
to the heroes of the sports world, and they let me down. I purchase a sure-win stock, and it loses money. Even the pillars of
the church let me down. "Where, oh where is my stability,"
cries out modern man. Everywhere he looks he is deceived. He
sees changes on the horizon and isn't sure what lies ahead.

Even though our stability is shaken in the present, God
promises, in Isaiah 33:6 that He will always be the same—
never wavering.

Change becomes a factor in all of our lives. If not today,
then surely tomorrow or the next day. Isn't it wonderful to
know that when change comes we can go to God's Word to
find strength to see us through another situation? Let's not
wait for the storm to hit before we seek verses that comfort
and direct. Let's be prepared when these days appear.

Today's Action

- ◆ Do you see any future changes for you and your family?
  What are they? What verses will help you get through
  them?

Prayer

*Father God, prepare in our hearts those Scriptures that will get
us through changes. Amen.*

Thank You, God, for quiet places far from life's crowded ways, where our hearts find true contentment and our souls fill up with praise.

Yes, There Is a Difference

For Thou didst form my inward parts; Thou didst weave me in my mother's womb, I will give thanks to Thee, for I am fearfully and wonderfully made.

—Psalm 139:13

A few months ago our local ABC affiliate was promoting a documentary special that reflected their latest research findings. They were going to give the viewer the latest evidence that men and women are made differently. I looked at Emilie and she looked at me, then we both laughed. Where had these producers been the last 2,000 years?

We don't pride ourselves as intellectual geniuses but we certainly had a grasp on this topic. The media for so long has tried to tell us that there aren't any differences, that we're all the same. Unfortunately, much of the Christian community has bought into this lie. Thus a woman can't comprehend why her husband doesn't look at situations the same way she does. She wonders, "Why isn't he sensitive?" "Why doesn't he like to go shopping with me?" "Why does work seem more important to him than family?"

Men and women are different in many ways: in physiology and anatomy, in thought patterns, in cultural roles and expectations. For the most part these differences are the result of God's design. Genesis 1:27 reads, "And God created man in His own image, in the image of God He created him; male and female He created them."

Men and women, as different as they are, are made in God's image. God called this creation "good." King David remarked that it was wonderful. A Christian husband and wife can move into their marriage relationship with the confidence that God has put each person on the earth for a special purpose. Our differences are by God's design.

As Christian men and women, we are (and ever will be) different. As we incorporate God's attitude toward our differences, we will enjoy a house "filled with all precious and pleasant riches" (Proverbs 24:4). These rewards are:

- positive attitudes
- mutual respect
- good relationships
- depth of character
- pleasant memories

We have a choice. We can live in a war zone fueled by our differences, or we can understand and accept our differences.

Perhaps the greatest enemy of living in harmony is pride. God hates pride, yet we seem to struggle against it in everything we do. We must break down the walls that our differences erect so we can enjoy the rewards that "understanding" promises.

Today's Action

- Do something with your wife that you don't normally do, an activity that reflects your acceptance of her differences.

Prayer

Father God, I'm so glad You didn't make everyone like me. Differences among us is what makes life so interesting. Amen.

Financially Secure

❏
❏
❏

—————◇—————

I n our book *The Fifteen-Minute Money Manager*, Emilie and I lay out some basic principles that will lead a couple or an individual to financial freedom. We emphasized three principles:

◆ God owns everything; He merely loans it to us as we show Him our ability to be good stewards of what He owns.

◆ Money is a resource used to accomplish other goals and obligations you have for your life purpose. Money is never an end by itself.

◆ Have less expenditures than you do income and you will have extra money to save, invest, and share. This will give you financial independence.

There is a great amount of freedom when one knows and believes that God owns everything. It takes away the idea that "I did it all myself" and "I'm a self-made man." One of our goals (short and long term) needs to cover the financial aspects of our lives. The average person who understands these three concepts will over time become financially independent. I define success as "progressive realization of worthwhile goals." You have to be able to postpone immediate gratification.

Today's Action
◆ Establish a plan to make you and your family financially independent. Learn ways to make money grow little by little.

Prayer
Father God, please help me implement these principles so I can be a better steward of Your resources. Amen.

A Reverence for God

The fear of the LORD is the beginning of wisdom;
a good understanding have all those who do His
commandments; His praise endures forever.

—Psalm 111:10

———————◇———————

F
ear of the Lord" is a reverence for God expressed in submission to His will (Job 28:28, Ecclesiastes 12:13,
Proverbs 9:10, 15:33). It is also the starting point and essence of
wisdom. Wisdom is not acquired by a mechanical formula, but
through a right relationship with God. It seems that following
God's principles should be the obvious conclusion of our
thankfulness for all He's done for us.

In today's church world, many people have lost the concept of fearing God. The soft side of Christianity has preached
only the "love of God." We haven't balanced the scale by
teaching the other side of justice—fear, anger, wrath, and punishment. Just because some church pulpits don't teach it
doesn't make it less a reality. As with involvement with drugs,
alcohol, lust, and envy, we must respect the consequences of
our actions or we will be destroyed by their side effects. Our
check point on all these potential destroyers is to have a
proper respect for God. Only then will we be obedient to His
precepts and stay away from the fire of temptation.

Today's Action
♦ Exhibit a new respect for your all-powerful God.
Prayer
Father God, fill me with an awesome respect for You. I want to
be obedient to Your precepts. Amen.

Two Things to Do

Prove yourselves doers of the word, and not merely hearers who delude [deceive] themselves.

—James 1:22

————◇————

Susannah Wesley once said that there are two things you do with the gospel: one is you believe it and two you live it. I often think that living it is harder than believing it.

Our children look more at how we live our everyday lives than they do our mere belief. That means our example is very powerful. Our wisdom in guiding our children through those difficult teen years is one of the best measures of how much we love and value them. Even though moms also count, the love and value from dad is vital for our children to stay on course.

When my children were in high school, a good friend of theirs, Lynne, named me "King Venee." I was all knowledge to them. It was a nickname that has stuck, even 20 years later! The other night Emilie said that I am now more of a King Venee than when the kids were in high school. I've had 20 more years to make good decisions!

You won't be able to sell your kids on a double standard when it comes to the important issues of life. They will be more willing to follow what you *do* and what you *believe* than what you say.

No one else can be as good a father to your children as you. You are helping to build tomorrow's future.

Today's Action

♦ Live by what you do, not by what you say. Become your child's "King Venee."

Prayer

Father God, let me realize the magnitude of being a father. Help me live out my beliefs. Amen.

A Powerful Hope

> *Consider it all joy, my brethren, when you*
> *encounter various trials.*

> **—James 1:2**

———◇———

Throughout Scripture we read of victory through troubles and suffering. Helmut Thielicke, the great German pastor and theologian, testified to this kind of victory during the horrors of World War II. One author wrote:

> When Thielicke said, "We live by God's surprises," he had personally suffered under the Nazis. As a pastor he wrote to young soldiers about to die; he comforted mothers and fathers and children after the bombs killed their loved ones. He preached magnificent sermons week after week as bombs blew apart his church and the lives and dreams of his parishioners. He spoke of God not only looking in love at His suffering people, weeping with them as they were surrounded by flames, but of God's hand reaching into the flames to help them, His own hand scorched by the fires.
>
> From the depths of suffering and the wanton destruction during the Nazi regime, Thielicke held out a powerful Christian hope. To Germans disillusioned by the easily manipulated faith of their fathers, he quoted Peter Wust: "The great things happen to those who pray. But we learn to pray best in suffering."
>
> Prayer, suffering, joy, and the surprises of God . . . they are all tightly enmeshed. But most shrink from

the above statement, seeing suffering as the surest killer of both joy and "great things."

When we are rightly related to God, life is full of joyful uncertainty and expectancy.... We do not know what God is going to do next; He packs our lives with surprises all the time.

What a strange idea: "joyful uncertainty." Most of us view uncertainty as cause for anxiety, not joy. Yet this call to expectancy rings true. The idea of standing on tiptoe to see what God is going to do next can transform our way of seeing. Prayers go maddeningly unanswered as well as marvelously fulfilled. Prayer becomes the lens through which we begin to see from God's perspective.

Thielicke, along with the other historical pillars of the church, gives testimony that prayer becomes the lens through which we begin to see life from God's perspective.

Wouldn't it be wonderful if, when we got out of bed each morning, we stood on our tiptoes to see "out the window" and discover what God is going to do today? We would joyfully look forward to seeing what He was going to do next. When we see life like that, our cup will surely run over and life will be joyful. Our cup will always be full, and as we pour out its contents God will give us new refreshment to fill it full again. Lord, I want to experience that joy!

Today's Action

- ◆ Stand on your tiptoes to see what God is going to do today.

Prayer

Father God, help me learn to see life from Your perspective. Give me depth in my prayer life. Amen.

What to Count

Don't count how many years you've spent,
Just count the good you've done;
The times you've lent a helping hand,
The friends that you have won.
Count your deeds of kindness,
The smiles not the tears;
Count all the pleasures
That you've had
But never count the years.

Restoration and Refuge

His name will be called Wonderful, Counselor,
Mighty God, Eternal Father, Prince of Peace.

—Isaiah 9:6

❑
❑
❑

————◇————

W hat do you think of when you hear the name "Jesus"? Miracles? Salvation? Peace? Purpose? Joy? Power? Hope? All of these—and more? There is indeed something about that name, the name of the Almighty God who parted the Red Sea, raised Lazarus from the dead, and lives today in every believer.

And the fact that He lives today gives us hope and peace. As Isaiah wrote, "Of the increase of his government of peace there will be no end" (9:7 NIV). Life brings sorrow, broken hearts, health problems, financial difficulties, and many other hardships. But God gives us peace and hope for those times. Let yourself depend on God and find refuge and restoration in Him.

It helps some people to visualize putting all their problems and worries in a box, sealing the lid, laying it at Jesus' feet, and then walking away, never turning back. It also helps to realize that 80 percent of the things we worry about never happen anyway—and we can let Jesus take the remaining 20 percent. In response, He will give back to you 100 percent of His life and peace. In fact, He has done it already for you when He died on the cross of Calvary.

Jesus. There is indeed something about that name—and in Him you will find exactly what you need for today.

Today's Action

- ◆ Take one of God's names and praise Him for being that person. Then reel off 10 blessings that you're thankful for.

Prayer

Father God, in each of Your names in Scripture help me discover who You are. Amen.

A Formula for Life

Seek first His Kingdom and His righteousness;
and all these things shall be added to you.

—Matthew 6:33

We live in a very anxious society. Many of us are more worried about tomorrow than today. We bypass all of today's contentment because of what might happen tomorrow. In Matthew 6:31 we read that the early Christians asked the same basic questions we do:

- ◆ What shall we eat?
- ◆ What shall we drink?
- ◆ What shall we wear?

Jesus tells them in verse 34, "Do not be anxious for tomorrow; for tomorrow will care for itself. Each day has enough trouble of its own." The formula Jesus gives for establishing the right priorities of life is in today's verse. Emilie and I have used this verse as our mission verse for the last 42 years. Each day we claim these two instructions:

- ◆ Seek *His* kingdom
- ◆ Seek *His* righteousness

Often we are overwhelmed by having too many things to do. Life offers many good choices on how to schedule our time. But we all have only 24 hours a day. How are we to use these hours effectively? When we seek these first, God's kingdom then His righteousness, we find that our day takes shape, and we can say "yes" we will do that or "no" we will not do that. When we begin to set priorities, we determine what is important and what isn't, and how much time we are willing to give each activity. The Bible gives us guidelines:

- ◆ our personal relationships with Him (Matthew 6:33; Philippians 3:8).

- ◆ our time for home and family (Genesis 2:24; Psalm 127:3; 1 Timothy 3:2-5).

- ◆ our time for work (1 Thessalonians 4:11,12).

- ◆ our time for ministry and community activities (Colossians 3:17).

We cannot do all the things that come our way. Emilie and I have a saying that helps us when we have too many choices: "Say no to the good things; say yes for the best."

Don't be afraid to say no. If you have established Matthew 6:33 as one of the key verses in your life you can very quickly decide whether a particular opportunity will help you—

- ◆ seek God's kingdom;
- ◆ seek God's righteousness.

After learning to say "no" easily, you can begin to major on the big things of life and not get bogged down by minor issues or situations.

Today's Action

- ◆ Say no to something that sounds good, but doesn't fit into today's goals.

Prayer

Father God, help me discern Your will, so I will know when to say no and when to say yes. Amen.

You Have Talents!

Well done, good and faithful servant! You have been faithful with a few things; I will put you in charge of many things. Come and share your master's happiness.

—Matthew 25:21

—————◇—————

G od calls us to use our talents faithfully for Him. What talents has God given you? Too often we think of talents as fully developed abilities, but it is only as we cultivate our talents that they become mature. Furthermore, we must be willing to take the risk of using our talents.

Consider what God is saying specifically to you in the "talent" parable Jesus told in Matthew 25:14-30. In today's parable, the first two servants were willing to take a risk. Not only did they receive a 100-percent return for their efforts, but their master praised them (see today's verse). Note that despite their different talents and abilities the first two servants received the same reward, indicating that God requires us to be faithful in the use of our abilities, whatever they are. If you want to be successful in God's eyes, you must first be faithful with the responsibilities He gives you. Then He will put you in charge of many things.

Is there a talent that people tell you you are good at, but you just shrug it off as not being good enough? Do you think no one could be blessed by your talent? This passage tells you to take the risk. Volunteer for that position, write that book, sign up for that class, offer to help with that project. Listen to God today as He calls you to the life of adventure that comes with using the gifts He's given you. Don't limit God.

Now let's look at the warning to those people who don't use their talents. The third servant was afraid. Unwilling to take a risk with his one talent, he buried it in the ground.

Because there wasn't a return on his "investments," this third servant is condemned for his sloth and indifference.

Are you burying your talents? God will hold you responsible for what you do with your talents, with your life. God wants you to take the risk of using the talents He has given you. Take the first step today, and you'll be amazed at what God can do! And one day you'll be blessed when you hear God say, "Well done, good and faithful servant!"

Today's Action

- Step out and take a risk. Use your talents!

Prayer

Father God, I'm nervous about taking this step, but You promised You would not let me fall. I take You on Your word. Amen.

Changing Course

One foggy night, the captain of a large ship saw what appeared to be another ship's lights approaching in the distance. This other ship was on a course that would mean a head-on crash. Quickly the captain signaled to the approaching ship, "Please change your course 10 degrees west." The reply came blinking back through the thick fog, "You change your course 10 degrees east."

Indignantly the captain pulled rank and shot a message back to the other ship, "I'm a sea captain with 35 years of experience. You change your course 10 degrees west!" Without hesitation the signal flashed back, "I'm a seaman fourth class. You change your course 10 degrees east!"

Enraged and incensed, the captain realized that within minutes they would crash head-on so he blazed his final warning back to the fast-approaching ship: "I'm a 50,000 ton freighter. You change your course 10 degrees west!" The simple message winked back, "I'm a lighthouse. You change..."

Have you come to a fork in the road of your marriage? Because of past experiences, you or your wife may not want to budge from your current position. I petition today for both of you to come to grips with what's holding you a prisoner and that you be set free by Christ's atonement for your sins.

Once you have come to grips with this issue the other related adjustments may seem minor. It makes no difference how you do some things, but this spiritual change will become a pivotal point around which all the other changes can take place.

One of the guiding principles when it comes to change is found in Ephesians 5:21, "And be subject to one another...." It's important to talk over conflicts and changes with your spouse. It's also crucial to take into consideration the differences you and your spouse have in how you like to implement new directions. Our tendency is to want to serve rather than to be served. Each day Emilie and I ask, "How can we serve each other today?" With that daily attitude we are free to serve each other in a mature, godly fashion. Anything less than that will let selfishness and pride enter into our lives, which will ultimately create an unwillingness to make changes.

Be willing to change your course rather than have your own way and ram into the lighthouse.

Today's Action

- Resolve those differences that can be, and continue to pray for those that can't.

Prayer

Father God, thank You for a heart that is willing to be flexible and a willingness to make proper changes in life. Amen.

The Peacemaker

If a house is divided against itself, that house will not be able to stand.

—Mark 3:25

———◇———

"A house divided against itself cannot stand," Abraham Lincoln said in his acceptance speech for his nomination for the United States Senate. "Either the opponents of slavery will arrest the further spread of it and place it where the public mind shall rest in the belief that it is in the course of ultimate extinction, or its advocates will push it forward, till it shall become alike lawful in all the states, old as well as new—north as well as south."

Lincoln's stand against slavery and for the equality of peoples eventually resulted in his defeat in the senate election, but Lincoln responded philosophically: "Though I now sink out of view and shall be forgotten, I believe I have made some marks which will tell for the cause of civil liberty long after I am gone." Well Lincoln certainly didn't "sink out of view"! Later as president of the United States, he worked to bring together those who had been at war and to heal the hurts that had divided the nation and some families within it.

Many families today are divided and need to be brought together; many hurts in families need to be healed. I've watched this happen in Emilie's family. Her two aunts hadn't spoken to each other for 10 years. The initial disagreement, as slight as it may have been, became unbridgeable. Neither would apologize or admit to being wrong. Having watched this go on for a long time, Emilie decided that she was going to be the peacemaker. She arranged a family gathering and invited both aunts. After a short time, the two began to open up and talk to each other. By the end of the evening, they had made amends, and they were able to enjoy the last 15 years of their lives together.

Maybe such division exists in your family. If so, know that the warning in today's Scripture is for you. If a family remains divided it will collapse. What can you do to help bring unity to your family? What can you do to help healing come to your home? Whatever steps you decide to take, you'll need a lot of patience and many prayers. As you seek God's blessing on your attempts to rebuild your home, ask Him to give you wisdom and understanding. It will take time to rebuild what has been destroyed by division, so don't expect instant results. Be willing to walk by faith, not by sight, and pray earnestly for unity each step of the way.

Today's Action

♦ Reach out and be a peacemaker when division exists.

Prayer

Father God, as I move out to be a peacemaker, go before me and heal the wounds that prevail. Amen.

Your success as a family, our success as a society, depends not on what happens in the White House, but in what happens inside your house.

—*Barbara Bush*

Adopted!

*I came that they might have life, and might have
it more abundantly.*

—John 10:10

---◇---

Our son, Brad, and daughter-in-law, Maria, were really
excited as they waited for their first child, Bradley Joe
II, to be born. Maria worked hard to take care of that baby
even then. She ate right, exercised regularly, and got plenty of
rest. It never occurred to me that Bradley Joe was not in the
absolutely safest place possible during those nine months
before he was born.

Then one evening Emilie and I attended a service at an
Evangelical Free Church in Fullerton, California. Pastor Chuck
Swindoll introduced the speaker for the evening, a man
named Ravi Zacharias. His opening statement was: "The most
dangerous place for a young child today is in his mother's
womb." He was talking about our country's abortion epi-
demic. Children are being thrown away like trash, right in our
own cities. As a society, we no longer view children as "a gift
of the LORD" (Psalm 127:3), much less a miracle of the
Almighty God.

After a bout with cancer, our niece Becky and her husband, George, adopted a son. God allowed a child to be born
to another woman so Becky and George could be parents. This
child is another gift from God. He wasn't thrown away in an
abortion clinic; instead, he was adopted into a family who
wanted a child.

And that's exactly what God offers us. He wants to adopt
us into His family. We are not God's throwaways. We are His
much-loved children for whom He sent His Son Jesus. Jesus

165

came to give us life (John 10:10), and then He went to the cross so that we will never have to suffer the punishment of sin.

Our relationship with Jesus is the only way we can fill the God-shaped void in our spirits. Nothing else in the world can fill that vacuum—although we try to fill it with work, recreation, busyness, toys, sex, alcohol, and many other things. The spiritual void can be experienced as mental, emotional, or even physical problems. When those problems arise, they help us acknowledge the hunger for God that is at their root. Then we can find fulfillment, contentment, and the abundant life Jesus promised.

Have you let yourself be adopted as God's child? Are you experiencing the abundant life He offers His sons and daughters?

Today's Action

♦ Go out today and live life abundantly (be joyful in the process).

Prayer

Father God, help me live the abundant life. Amen.

Reflecting Acceptance

Now to Him who is able to do exceeding abun-
dantly beyond all that we ask or think, accord-
ing to the power that works within us...to Him
be the glory.

—Ephesians 3:20

———◇———

P eter Foster was a Royal Air Force pilot. RAF men were the cream of the crop of England—the brightest, healthi-est, most confident and dedicated, and often the most hand-some men in the country. When they walked the streets in their decorated uniforms, the population treated them as roy-als. All eyes turned their way. Women envied those who were fortunate enough to walk beside a man in air-force blue.

However, the scene in London was far from romantic, because the Germans were attacking relentlessly. Fifty-seven consecutive nights they bombed London. In waves of 250, some 1,500 bombers would come each evening and pound the city.

The RAF Hurricanes and Spitfires that pilots like Foster flew looked like mosquitoes pestering the huge German bombers. The Hurricane was agile and effective, yet it had one fatal design flaw. The single propeller engine was mounted in front, a scant foot or so from the cockpit, and the fuel lines snaked alongside the cockpit toward the engine. In a direct hit, the cockpit would erupt into an inferno of flames. The pilot could bail out, but in the one or two seconds it took him to find the lever, heat would melt off every feature of his face; his nose, his eyelids, his lips, often his cheeks.

The RAF heroes that survived this experience would undergo a series of 20 to 40 surgeries to refashion what once was their face. Plastic surgeons worked miracles, yet what remained of the face was essentially a scar.

Peter Foster became one of these "downed pilots." After numerous surgical procedures, what remained of his face was indescribable. The mirror he peered into daily couldn't hide the facts. As the day for his release from the hospital grew closer, so did Peter's anxiety about being accepted by his family and friends.

He knew that one group of airmen with similar injuries had returned home only to be rejected by their wives and girlfriends. Some of the men were divorced by wives who were unable to accept this new image of their husbands. Some men became recluses, refusing to leave their houses.

In contrast, there was another group who returned home to families who gave loving assurance of acceptance and continued worth. Many became executives and professionals, leaders in their communities.

Peter Foster was in that second group. His girlfriend assured him that nothing had changed except a few millimeters of thick skin. She loved him, not his facial membrane, she assured him. The two were married just before Peter left the hospital.

"She became my mirror," Peter said of his wife. "She gave me a new image of myself. Even now, regardless of how I feel, when I look at her she gives me a warm, loving smile that tells me I am O.K.," he relates confidently.

We reflect to our mates and children acceptance or rejection by our verbal and nonverbal communications. They derive part of their worth from how we relate to them. In order for our family members to feel worthy, they need people around them that reflect acceptance.

Negative reflection builds fear. All around us we can see a nation built on fear as more and more teenagers at school or at local malls are subjected to harsh situations—even violence. They radiate the dullness of living with fear.

Ephesians 4:29 says, "Let no unwholesome word proceed from your mouth, but only a word as is good for edification ... that it may give grace to those who hear." As your wife and children look and listen to you, are they free from fear because they know you value their places in the family structure? Reassure them each day through your words *and* deeds that you really love them.

Today's Action

- Practice the basic principle in communication found in Ephesians 4:29.

Prayer

Father God, I want to be uplifting with my words toward my family. Give me a daily nudge. Amen.

Honored by God

But Noah found favor in the eyes of the Lord. . . .
Thus Noah did; according to all that God had
commanded him.

—Genesis 6:8,22

———————◇———————

I f you were to pick up today's paper, you'd probably find a
story about someone being honored for something he or she
did. It seems that the accomplishment of someone in government, sports, medicine, education, theater, or music is acknowledged by peers or even the world in general all the time.
People finding favor with people is not unusual.

Have you ever thought about how much richer it would
be to have God find favor with you? It's awesome to think of
our holy God finding favor in us human beings, but He does.

Noah lived in a sin-filled world much like ours today.
(Human beings haven't changed much over the centuries—we
just call "sin" something else.) Despite the wickedness around
him, Noah lived a godly life that was pleasing to God.

It's important to realize that Noah didn't find favor *because*
of his individual goodness, but because of his *faith* in God. You
and I are judged by that same standard—are we faithful and
obedient to God?

Although Noah was upright and blameless before God, he
wasn't perfect. Genuine faith is not always perfect faith. But
despite his human failings, Noah walked with God (Genesis
6:9). The circumstances of Noah's life could have blocked his
fellowship with God, but his heart attitude enabled him to
find favor with God.

Are you seeking favor with God or the favor and honor of
people? Noah wanted only to please God. When you go to
God and admit you are a sinner, you are pleasing God. At that
time, you will experience God's grace and move into a closer

relationship with Jesus Christ. May you, like Noah, find favor in God's sight.

Today's Action

- Do something today to find favor with God (do it under grace, not under law).

Prayer

Father God, help me to be faithful and obedient to You so that I might find favor with You. Amen.

Never Forsaken

The LORD knows the days of the blameless; and their inheritance will be forever.

—Psalm 37:1-40

———◇———

I don't know if you're like I am, but when I look at the local news events on television and in the newspaper, I see very little hope for the future. I get concerned for my children and grandchildren, and even for my great-grandchildren. I see moral decay from what I cherished by being raised in the '50s. When I go by a high school, visit a mall, listen to the music of the youth, see the art of the masses, or witness the violence of the movies, I scream in my soul, *Stop!*

Then the Lord brings before me Psalm 37. In this passage David exhorts the righteous to trust in the Lord. Even when it looks like evil will overpower righteousness, God never abandons His children (verse 25). Though they may experience the heartaches of a sinful, fallen world, God's children are never forsaken. In fact, His blessings will extend to the next generation (verse 26).

During my quiet time with the Lord in this particular psalm, certain key phrases comfort me:

- Do not fret: be not envious (verse 1).
- Trust in the Lord, cultivate faithfulness (verse 3).
- Delight yourself in the Lord; He will give you abundantly the desires of your heart (verse 4).
- Commit your way to the LORD, trust also in Him (verse 5).
- Rest in the Lord; wait patiently (verse 7).
- Cease from anger; do not fret (verse 8).
- The humble will inherit the land (verse 11).

- Depart from evil (verse 27).
- Wait for the Lord (verse 34).

In verses 39 and 40 we read of the great blessings we receive as children of God: "The salvation of the righteous is from the LORD; He is [our] strength in time of trouble. And the LORD helps [us], and delivers [us]; He delivers [us] from the wicked and saves [us], because [we] take refuge in Him."

As I leave my time of prayer I am again able to face the negative issues of the day because David took time centuries ago to write this poetic psalm of comfort.

Today's Action

- Learn to trust, delight, commit, rest, be humble, and wait. Read and meditate on Psalm 37—one verse a day.

Prayer

Father God, give me assurance that righteousness still deflects evil, as it did centuries ago. Amen.

A Lasting Inheritance

I thank my God in all my remembrance of you.

—Philippians 1:3

❏
❏
❏

———◇———

I t was a warm, sunny day for January and two of our four grandchildren were helping us enjoy it. Ten-year-old Christine helped her Grammy Em cook dinner. Bevan and I raked the garden and picked oranges, avocados, and lemons off our trees.

As the afternoon progressed, we working "men" got hot and tired. We were really glad to see Emilie and Christine come up the hill with juice and snacks. We thanked them and headed for the bench that sits under a large shady avocado tree overlooking the grounds and the street in front of our home.

That night Emilie and I talked about our day with the grandchildren. "What does a PaPa and his seven-year-old grandson talk about on the bench under the big avocado tree?" Emilie asked.

"Oh," I replied, "boys talk just like you girls talk—but about boy things."

I had told Bevan, "Someday, when PaPa's in heaven and you drive down this street as a man, you'll look at this bench we are sitting on and remember the day that Grammy Em and Christine served us jam and toast with a glass of juice."

Then Bevan said, "Not only will I remember, but I will bring my son, and someday he will bring his son and point to the bench and tell him about the toast and jam we ate on the bench under that big avocado tree over there." Only seven years old, Bevan already understood something of the value of one generation sharing stories with the next.

What a privilege and responsibility we parents have—to be called to teach our children and grandchildren the story of God's love and the stories of Jesus, so that someday they will thank God for their memory of us and the stories we shared.

Today's Action

- Tell your children something they will remember long after you are gone.

Prayer

Father God, let me realize that I am raising present as well as future generations. Amen.

What families have in common the world around is that they are the place where people learn who they are and how to be that way.

—*Jean Illsley Clarke*

The Refiner

*And I will bring [them] through the fire, refine
them as silver is refined, and test them as gold
is tested. They will call My name, and I will
answer them.*

—Zechariah 13:9

————◇————

When times are hard, it's easy to ask, "Why, Lord?
Why do Your children suffer?" Job certainly had
every reason to ask that question. He loved and
obeyed God, but God gave Satan permission to test
him. That meant great suffering and loss for Job, but
he was a man with staying power. One reason his
faith in the Lord didn't waver was because his masculinity wasn't determined by what he owned, the
size of his home, the amount of his investments,
what he could do, the people he knew, the model of
donkey he rode, or his status in the community.
Job's masculinity and personhood were firmly rooted in who he was, alone and naked, before God.
And God is what makes men of all of us.

—Adapted from Stu Weber, *Tender Warrior*
(Multnomah 1993)

I n that process, God often uses suffering. My friends Glen
and Marilyn Heavilin, for instance, know the kind of suffering Job knew. They have lost three sons—one in crib death;
one twin by pneumonia; and the second twin by a teenage
drunk driver. Glen and Marilyn were tested, but they have
come through the refiner's fire. Today they use their experiences to glorify the name of the Lord.

Marilyn has written *Roses in December*, which is the story
of how they lost their sons. She has had the opportunity to
speak all over the country in high school auditoriums filled

with teenagers. There she shares her story and talks about life and death, chemical dependency, and God.

Did God know what He was doing when He chose the Heavilins? Of course. They have come forth as gold fired in the heat of life, and they are able to shine for Him. Their pain will never be gone, but they still minister. They've been very active in "Compassionate Friends," a support group for families who have experienced the death of children. God knew the path the Heavilins would take when they faced their tragic losses, and He's been there as their faith in Him has been purified.

Every one of us has experienced some kind of tragedy. It's not the specifics of the event that matter as much as how we handle it. Whatever loss you're dealing with and however you're being tested, you can be sure that others have been tested that way, too. So don't go through the testing alone. Trust in God, and find someone you can trust who will bear the burden with you. You, too, can and will come forth as gold.

Remember that Jesus knows your pain, and He is always with you to help you get through the tough times in life. Trust Him now. It's all part of the "coming forth as gold" that Job talks about.

Today's Action

- ◆ Think about how God might be using this pain and suffering in your life to help your Christian growth "come forth as gold."

Prayer

Father God, it hurts so much but I know I will come out stronger. Help me remember You are with me. Amen.

Never Alone

If any of you lacks wisdom, let him ask of God,
who gives to all generously....

—James 1:5

❑
❑
❑

———————◇———————

Some of you may not have a prayer life at all. Others of you may have a very vital prayer life. And some of you want to have a prayer life but are frustrated because you don't know how to incorporate prayer into your life or how to organize it. I was once in that position. I was fumbling in my prayer life because I didn't know the steps to take. One of the first things I had to learn was to trust God for my every care. Often in life I had been disappointed by those I trusted, but "One Set of Footprints" helped me realize that I was never alone.

One Set of Footprints

One night a man had a dream. In his dream he was walking along the beach with the Lord, when across the sky flashed all the events of his life. However, for each scene he noticed two sets of footprints in the sand, one belonging to him and the other to the Lord. When the last scene had flashed before him, he looked back at the footprints and noticed that many times along the path there was only one set of footprints in the sand. He also noticed that this happened during the lowest and saddest times of his life.

This really bothered him, so he said to the Lord, "You promised that once I decided to follow You, You would walk with me all the way, but I noticed that during the roughest times of my life there was only one set of footprints. I don't understand why You deserted me when I needed You the most."

The Lord replied, "My precious child, I love you and I would never leave you. During those times of trial and suffering when you saw only one set of footprints, it was then that I carried you."

—Author unknown

You see, God is *always* with us. When the times are the lowest, that's when He picks us up and carries us. Isn't that wonderful? Some of us have experienced that, some of us are being carried through rough situations or problems in our lives right now. It's great to know that we can pray to the Lord, and He is with us and will carry us when we are in despair or feel overwhelmed.

If you are not used to praying, begin with little steps. Talk to God as you would a friend. Your prayer doesn't have to be long or fancy. God wants to hear from your heart.

Today's Action

♦ Memorize the Lord's Prayer found in Matthew 6:1-13.

Prayer

Father God, be patient with me while I step out in the area of prayer. Help me turn to You in times of trouble. Amen.

The Lost Mitt

*And the LORD will continually guide you, and
satisfy your desire in scorched places, and give
strength to your bones; and you will be like...a
spring of water whose waters never fail.*

—Isaiah 58:11

❑
❑
❑

---◇---

I t was our son Brad's first real-leather baseball mitt. I taught
him how to break it in with special oil. The oil is rubbed
into the pocket of the glove, then Brad tossed his baseball from
hand to hand to form a pocket just right for him. Brad loved
his mitt and worked for hours each day to make it fit him just
right. He was so happy to have such a special glove for his
baseball practices and games.

One afternoon after practice one of the older boys asked to
see his mitt. He looked it over, then threw it into a grassy field.
Brad ran to find his special possession, but he couldn't find it.
Nowhere was his mitt to be found. With a frightened, hurt
heart, Brad came home in tears.

After he told his mom the story she encouraged him by
saying that it had to be there somewhere.

"I'll go with you Brad, and we'll search the lot until we
find it," Emilie promised.

"But Mom, I did search the lot, and it's not there," replied
Brad tearfully.

So I said, "Brad, let's pray and ask God to help us." By
now it was beginning to get dark and we needed to hurry, so
in the car we jumped and as I drove Brad and Emilie to the
baseball field we asked God to please guide our steps directly
to the glove. Parking quickly, we headed for the field. Again
we asked God to point us in the right direction. Immediately
Brad ran into the tall grass of the field and there, about 20 feet
away "thumb up" was Brad's glove.

God answers our prayers! Sometimes it's wait, yes, or later. For Brad, that day it was yes. God said, in essence, "I'll direct you to find the mitt of this young boy whose heart was broken because of a bully kid and a lost glove."

Do you have a "lost glove" today? Go before God and praise Him for the promise He gave us in Isaiah 58:11. If God says it, believe it. He *will* direct you and guide you. Open your heart to listen to what His direction is, then press ahead. The grass may seem too tall to see very far, but trust the Lord and keep walking until you feel in your heart the peace you desire. God may lead in a direction you least expect, but step forward with confidence in the Lord.

Today's Action

◆ Step out in faith that you will find your "lost glove."

Prayer

Father God, help me walk in the field of grass letting You continually guide me. Amen.

In the Lord's Tent

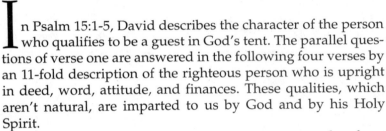

In Psalm 15:1-5, David describes the character of the person who qualifies to be a guest in God's tent. The parallel questions of verse one are answered in the following four verses by an 11-fold description of the righteous person who is upright in deed, word, attitude, and finances. These qualities, which aren't natural, are imparted to us by God and by his Holy Spirit.

Let's see what we can learn from this great psalm about the person who may dwell in the Lord's tent:

1. He walks blameless (verse 2).
2. He does what is righteous (verse 2).
3. He speaks the truth from his heart (verse 2).
4. He has no slander on his tongue (verse 3).
5. He does his neighbor no harm (verse 3).
6. He casts no slur on his friends (verse 3).
7. He despises an evil man (verse 4).
8. He honors those who fear the Lord (verse 4).
9. He keeps his oath even when it hurts (verse 4).
10. He lends his money without interest (verse 5).
11. He doesn't accept a bribe (verse 5).

These are honorable characteristics! We certainly can appreciate the virtue of this type of person. However, many times we look upon the life of a righteous person and say to ourselves, "It must be easy for him to be a Christian. He evidently doesn't have the struggles with sin like I do!" Yet all people who are trying to live a righteous life must choose each day to serve the Lord. It isn't easy for any of us. We must decide moment by moment to do what is right.

David closes this psalm by stating, "He who does these things will never be shaken" (verse 5). What a great promise. Live it with great faith.

Today's Action

- ◆ Inventory your level of character and see what areas you need to work on. Write down 3 to 5 things you could do to improve these areas.

Prayer

Father God, I willfully decide today to believe and live the Scriptures of old, precept by precept and line by line. Amen.

I Love You

Jesus said to Simon Peter..."Do you love Me more than these?"

—John 21:15

❏
❏
❏

---◇---

It seems as though we go through life wondering if our wives, our children, and our friends love us. We feel insecure about the other people in our lives, and we're not sure where we stand. Even though we tell and show the people in our lives that we love them, they don't seem to catch the answer because they're always reaching out to test our love for them.

Sometimes our children wear crazy clothes, put rings in their ears, color their hair strange colors, or use foul language to see if we really love them.

In our passage today Jesus asks Peter three times whether Peter really loves Him (verses 15,16,17).

I believe that these basic questions correspond to Peter's three denials of Jesus (see John 13:38). Jesus in all of his love, wanted to give Peter a second chance to follow Him. He didn't want Peter to go all through life with the stigma of denying Jesus. He wanted Peter to know that he was forgiven for his wrongdoing, and he could have a valuable ministry in spreading the gospel throughout the world.

But before Peter was able to confirm his love for Jesus, Jesus stated in John 21:18,19 that the decision was going to cost him a price. (In fact, according to church tradition, Peter and his wife were crucified upside down approximately 40 years later. After stating there would be a price for following Him, Jesus said, "Follow me," and Peter did.

Yes, love has its price—not always to the extreme of Peter's—but a cost of time, energy, commitment, money, and devotion. Selfish people take without giving back, but a true lover of people is always giving and giving and giving.

Is there someone in your life who is asking this very basic question: "Do you love me?" What is your reply?

Today's Action

- ◆ Let your family know again that you love them. Look them straight in the eyes when you tell them.

Prayer

Father God, let my words and actions show those around me that I love them. Amen.

Celebration

Knowing that this world can weigh us down and wear us out, God encourages us to take and make time for celebrating.

Keys to Communication

———◇———

Two of my very favorite relatives were Uncle Saul and Auntie Phyllis. For years, before Uncle Saul passed away, they would tell about a certain event and they would always disagree on how it happened: they didn't go by boat, they flew; they didn't see the movie, they saw the play; they served chicken, not beef; it was snowing, not the sun shining. Regardless of the subject they disagreed.

After awhile we would say, "Five o'clock, six o'clock, what difference does it make?" Yet they would continue to correct each other on the details of the story. Fortunately they would also smile and laugh and not take it personally, but we knew they would never agree on anything.

Marriage experts tell us that the number-one cause for divorce in America today is lack of communication. Everyone is born with one mouth and two ears—the basic tools for communication. But evidently possessing the physical tools for communication is not enough. Couples must learn how to use their mouths and ears properly for true communication to take place. Since God created marriage for companionship, completeness, and communication, we can be sure that He will also provide us with the resources for fulfilling His design.

There are three partners in a Christian marriage: husband, wife, and Jesus Christ. In order for healthy communication to exist between husband and wife, there must be proper communication between all three partners. If there is a breakdown in dialog between any two members, the breakdown will automatically affect the third member of the partnership. Dwight

Small says: "Lines open to God invariably open to one another, for a person cannot be genuinely open to God and closed to his mate.... God fulfills His design for Christian marriage when lines of communication are first opened to Him." If you and your mate are having difficulty communicating, the first area to check is your individual devotional life with God.

Whenever Emilie and I suffer a breakdown in relating to one another, it is usually because one of us is not talking with God on a regular basis. When both of us are communicating with God regularly through prayer and the study of His Word, we enjoy excellent communication with each other.

In his book *Communication: Key to Your Marriage*, Norm Wright gives an excellent definition of communication: "Communication is a process (either verbal or nonverbal) of sharing information with another person in such a way that he understands what you are saying. *Talking* and *listening* and *understanding* are all involved in the process of communication."

As couples we need to spend more time on listening and understanding than upon talking.

Today's Action

♦ Practice the skills of listening.

Prayer

Father God, since You gave me two ears, let me listen twice as much as I speak. Amen.

The Faithful Slave

...that they should seek God, if perhaps they might grope for Him and find Him, though He is not far from each one of us.

—Acts 17:27

❏
❏
❏

---◇---

E ach of us has a unique story on how we found God. None is as unique as General Naaman's found in 2 Kings 5:1-16. This general had taken captive a slave girl from Israel, and she waited on his wife. This young maiden was concerned about the general's leprosy. She told her mistress that Naaman should find the prophet of God in Israel. She knew that if he found the prophet he would also find her God.

We never hear again about this faithful slave girl, but we know that Naaman found the prophet and did as he commanded. He bathed seven times in the Jordan River and was healed from his disease. He knew the miracle was from the true God. This all happened because a young slave girl was so concerned about his well-being that she directed him to a place where he could meet the real God.

God often uses ordinary people to lead the way. God isn't far away, and He wants all of us to find Him. When we come to Jesus, we are healed and made whole.

Bring your heavy burdens, your sins, your illnesses to Him and expect a miracle. Jesus is not far away.

Today's Action

♦ Point someone to God—share your faith.

Prayer

Father God, thank You for sending Jesus so He can wash away my sins with His blood. Amen.

The Purpose of Life

I press on toward the goal for the prize of the upward call of God in Christ Jesus.

—Philippians 3:14

❑
❑
❑

---◇---

A courageous statement was made by a man who, in struggling to understand the death of his loved one, stated, "I still do not see the purpose. I struggle, but I don't give up. Somehow I feel that in my very struggle with this I am choosing to say that there is meaning and purpose."

As Christians our lives have purpose. We weren't planted here for just a certain length of time; there is more to life than being alive. In John 10:10 Jesus states that He came so we might have abundant life. We should live life to the fullest, and we should reflect Christ by our lifestyle. When we understand life we will no longer struggle with death. A great promise regarding this principle is found in John 11:25,26, when Jesus said to Martha, "I am the resurrection and the life; he who believes in Me shall live even if he dies, and everyone who lives and believes in Me shall never die."

Do you believe this? How much you believe and live this promise determines how you will face life and death.

Today's Action

◆ Write out a "life statement of purpose." Share this with your wife.

Prayer

Father God, I know You came to give me life abundantly. I want to live life so that I reflect Your love to those around me. Amen.

Bearing the Burdens

For God is not unjust so as to forget your work and the love which you have shown toward His name, in having ministered and in still ministering.

—Hebrews 6:10

---◇---

The well-known author A.C. Dixon told the story of Joanna Ambrosius, the wife of a poor farmer who lived in the German Empire during the latter part of the nineteenth century. She and her husband spent many long hours in the fields, so she knew little of the outside world. But she had the soul of the poet. With her hope in God, she wrote down the thoughts that filled her heart. She had great sympathy for the struggling people around her, and her mother-heart expressed its joys and sorrows in poetry.

Somehow, a bit of verse she had written found its way into print and, later, into the hands of the empress of Germany. The royal lady was so impressed by the beauty of what she read that she asked that the author be located. Learning of Joanna and her meager lifestyle, the empress expressed her love for the woman by supplying her immediate needs and by giving her a pension for life.

Emilie and I were conducting a seminar in a small town in central Georgia, when we noticed a particular man who was really working hard on a late Friday afternoon to make the church just right for the 400 ladies coming to our Saturday women's conference. We were very impressed by how diligently he worked, so we went up to him and asked, "What do you do around here?" His response was classic. He stated, "No one knows until I don't do what they think I should do."

There are many such workers in our churches. We need to tell those workers who work in obscurity that they are important to the body of Christ. God observes everything a person does to help bear the burdens of others—and He will reward him or her. His eternal pension is guaranteed.

Remember, God sees each of our labors of love.

Today's Action

- ◆ Tell people who are serving in obscurity that you appreciate their hard work.

Prayer

Father God, thank You for remembering all those who serve in obscurity. Amen.

Honey, Take Out the Trash

Do nothing from selfishness or empty conceit,
but with humility of mind let each of you regard
one another as more important than himself.

—Philippians 2:3

———————◇———————

Not long ago Emilie and I had the good fortune to visit Canada and the town of Red Deer. Red Deer is a farming community on the flat plains of Alberta Province halfway between Calgary and Edmonton—a delightful spot any time, but strong Arctic winds in winter make the area very cold.

After landing at the airport and clearing customs, we were met by Val Day, one of our hostesses for the weekend. As she drove us north to Red Deer, Val spoke modestly, but with the unmistakable pride of a mother and wife about her children and her husband, Stockwell. She explained that her husband, who was in politics, would be home from the cabinet sessions in Edmonton over the weekend. That was the routine when the government was in session. Stockwell leaves home late Sunday afternoon, stays in his apartment in Edmonton through Thursday, drives back home to his Red Deer office Friday, spends the weekend with his family, and then starts the routine all over again late Sunday afternoon.

I very much looked forward to meeting Stockwell, the Minister of Labor for Alberta Province. As the weekend neared, I heard all kinds of positive things about this very fine Christian politician. He was interviewed on TV during the six o'clock news, and the newspaper printed several statements made by the Honorable Day during this session.

On Friday evening we were invited to the Days' home for dinner. After Emilie and I arrived and introductions were made, we enjoyed a barbecue on the patio with the Day family and other guests. Emilie and I knew we were in the home of someone special—but for other reasons than you might expect. This man was tremendously respected by the people in his province, but what impressed us more was that his family was a high priority for him. This man of God is the head of a family that lives out love. They share a sense of humor, appreciation of one another, and mutual respect. It was a pleasure to share the evening with them.

After Emilie's seminar on Saturday, Stockwell and Val drove us back to the airport so we could leave early Sunday morning. During the drive, I asked Stockwell a question I often ask successful Christian men. "Stockwell," I asked, "this week I have heard your name spoken with high admiration. I have seen the high regard your voters have for you, and I've heard you addressed by the title 'Honorable.' How do you stay humble and keep a proper perspective on who you are as a child of God?"

Without a moment's hesitation Stockwell replied, "When I get home on Friday afternoon, I give Val a hug and then she very matter-of-factly says, 'Honey, please take out the trash.' With that simple request, I am back down to earth. I'm reminded that I am a husband and father first and all other titles are secondary to my main earthly responsibilities."

Today's Action

◆ Take out the trash without having to be asked.

Prayer

Father God, make me realize that all good things come from above, and I'm just a vessel of your love. Amen.

Confident Living

Home is the one place in all this world where hearts are sure of each other. It is the place of confidence. It is the place where we tear off that mask of guarded and suspicious coldness which the world forces us to wear in self-defense, and where we pour out the unreserved communication of full and confiding hearts. It is the spot where expressions of tenderness gush out without any dread of sensation of awkwardness and without any dread of ridicule.

—Frederick W. Robertson

Precious Treasure

*But we have this treasure in earthen vessels,
that the surpassing greatness of the power may
be of God and not from ourselves.*

—2 Corinthians 4:7

---◇---

In today's Scripture, we read that we are "jars of clay" (earthen vessels) and that we hold the great treasure of the gospel within. Simply stated, Christianity is Jesus Christ—the treasure—residing in the Christian, a clay pot. And God trusts us, even commands us, to share that treasure with other people. Isn't it interesting that you and I hide our treasures in vaults and safe deposit boxes, but God trusts His treasure to a common clay pot? The only value our clay pot has is due to the treasure inside.

Do you honestly believe that God can use you to do the work He has called you to do for His kingdom? If we could believe and act on this promise, God's kingdom would reign more fully in our hearts, our homes, our churches, our cities, our country, and the world.

We men are to step forward and be the spiritual leaders in our homes. We are to gather our families together and share the treasure God has entrusted to us.

Today's Action

- ◆ Meditate on this: "In what parts of your life do you think God wants to use you for His kingdom?"

Prayer

Father God, don't let me hide my treasure in an earthen vessel. I want others around me to see what a precious treasure I have. Amen.

The Privilege of Close Fellowship

...so that Christ may dwell in your hearts through faith.

—Ephesians 3:17

A man was giving his testimony of salvation at an open-air meeting. God had miraculously changed him from a drunkard into a devoted Christian, and he now radiated the presence of Christ. As he spoke, someone in the crowd called out, "You talk as if Jesus Christ lived next door to you!" "No," answered the Christian, "He lives nearer than that—He dwells in my heart!"

Someone once observed that Christianity is not a religion but a relationship. Yes, this relationship with our Savior is much closer than our family ties. Through the presence of the Holy Spirit, *Jesus lives in every believer.*

Many religions of the world find it most difficult to know a God that says He will dwell in their hearts. I can remember when Emilie's Uncle Hy asked her if she talked to God today. She most assuredly replied, "Yes." That blew him away because in the Jewish faith one doesn't talk to God in such a personal way.

As Christians we can have close fellowship with Christ daily. His maximum assurance is that someday we will spend eternity with Him in heaven. Someone has written: "Near, so very near to God, nearer I could not be. For in the person of God's Son, I'm just as near as He." And that is so very true.

198

Today's Action

- ◆ Reach out to God and ask Him to dwell in your heart. If He does already, thank Him for being a caring, approachable God.

Prayer

Father God, may my heart be Your dwelling place. Let me clearly hear Your directions for my life. Amen.

The Freedom to Cry

But we proved to be gentle among you, as a nursing mother tenderly cares for her own children.

—1 Thessalonians 2:7

————◇————

When you think of the apostle Paul, you may think of the person who endured imprisonment, flogging, stoning, and shipwrecks (see 2 Corinthians 11:23-27), and that toughness was very much a part of the fiery apostle. But today's reading reveals his tender side. He describes himself as being gentle and tender. His hard-as-nails toughness didn't mean he was without his soft side.

I saw an example of a tough but tender man when Barbara Walters interviewed real-life hero "Stormin' Norman" Schwarzkopf, the four-star general who led the allied forces of Desert Storm to their Gulf War victory over Iraq. As this tough military man talked about the war, I saw tears in his eyes.

His interviewer noticed, too, and in her classic style, Barbara Walters asked, "Why, General, aren't you afraid to cry?" General Schwarzkopf replied without hesitation, "No, Barbara, I'm afraid of a man who won't cry!" This truly great man knows that being tough doesn't mean being insensitive or unfeeling or afraid to cry. No wonder soldiers gave their best when they served under his command. They knew the general cared about them; they could trust the man giving the orders. Men want leaders whose hearts can be touched by our situations and who touch our hearts as well.

Even today I vividly remember the encouragement that my high school and college basketball coaches would give me when they called me to the sidelines. As the coach explained the next play or the strategy for the game-winning maneuver, he would put his arm on my shoulder. That simple touch said, "Bob, I believe in you. You can make it happen."

Athletics can indeed be a real source of encouragement as boys travel the path to manhood. Granted, professional sports have become larger than life with the influx of the media dollars, but athletics remain a place where we can see the tender side of a tough athlete. That's what we're looking at when we see grown men jump into the arms of a coach or a teammate, two or more buddies high-fiving it, or a swarm of players jumping on top of the player who just made the big play. This childlike excitement is the tender side of the not-to-be-beaten athlete.

Are you able to give your friends pats on the back or bear hugs? We're all on the same team—God's—and we all need some encouragement as we head onto the field to make the big plays. We need each other if we're going to be victorious in this game called life.

Today's Action

◆ Give a friend a pat on the back and a hug.

Prayer

Father God, I stand before You humbly, recognizing that nothing should make me arrogant or high-minded. Amen.

Exiled

Build houses and live in them; and plant gar-
dens, and eat their produce.

—Jeremiah 29:5

————◇————

The prophet Jeremiah sent a letter to the Jews who had
been taken to Babylon in A.D. 597. He exhorted them to
live as normal a life as possible while in exile, and wait for
God's deliverance after 70 years.

Maybe you find yourself in exile (being where you don't
want to be, with people you don't want to be with, doing
things you don't want to do). This type of situation requires
that you decide how you will react. Will you state, "Woe is me,
I'm just not going to do anything" (a victim), or will your reply
be as Jeremiah's letter suggested, "Build houses and live in
them; and plant gardens and eat their produce" (victor)? Daily
we respond and answer the exile questions. In America today
we find two groups of people: the victims and the victors.
Almost every social, political, and economic question deals
with how to treat these two forces. We need to determine to do
the very best with today's situation whatever it might be. God
is here with us, and we're going to make it work.

All of us are given moments in time when we find ourselves in exile. How are we going to respond to new jobs, new
friends, new schools, or new churches? Exile points out to us
what really matters, and it permits us to strive again for what's
important in life.

Today's Action
- ◆ Decide to be a victor while in your exile.

Prayer
Father God, this exile is helping me depend upon You more each
day. Thank You. Amen.

Temptation Revealed

Do not enter the path of the wicked, and do not proceed in the way of evil men. Avoid it, do not pass by it; turn away from it and pass on.

—Proverbs 4:14,15

———————◇———————

Several artists were asked to illustrate their concepts of temptation. When their paintings were unveiled, some of them depicted man's attempt to achieve fame and fortune at any cost, while others pictured mankind's struggle against the alluring desires of the flesh. The prize-winning canvas, however, portrayed a pastoral scene in which a man was walking along a quiet country lane among inviting shade trees and lovely wild flowers. In the distance the way divided into two roads, the one leading to the right, the other to the left. The artist was seeking to convey the thought that sin's allurements are extremely subtle at first—just an innocent-looking fork in the road!

We are continually struggling with temptations in our lives. The ugly hands of sin reach out to grasp away from us any goodness we may have. Few of us would go straight from point A to B, but we will make smaller and easier choices toward evil before we finally give in to temptation. We must be aware of and sensitive to taking that first compromising step when we face temptation.

Today's Action
 ◆ Keep to the right when you come to the fork in the road.

Prayer
Father God, give me clear discernment when I come to a fork in the road. Help me turn toward Your righteousness. Amen.

God is the love of our lives, and He has called us in accordance with His purposes. He has promised us that all things will work together today for our good.

—*From Romans 8:28*

Planned Neglect

Daniel. . .continued kneeling on his knees three
times a day, praying and giving thanks before
His God, as he had been doing previously.

—**Daniel 6:10**

———◇———

In her book *A Practical Guide to Prayer*, Dorothy Haskins tells about a noted concert violinist who was asked the secret of her mastery of the instrument. The woman answered the question with two words: "Planned neglect." Then she explained. "There were many things that used to demand my time. When I went to my room after breakfast, I made my bed, straightened the room, dusted, and did whatever seemed necessary. When I finished my work, I turned to my violin practice. That system prevented me from accomplishing what I should on the violin. So I reversed things. I deliberately planned to neglect everything else until my practice period was complete. And that program of planned neglect is the secret of my success."

What priority does your quiet time have with the Lord? Do we fit it in sometime during the day or do we systematically give Him top priority? We have to plan our neglect of other things in order to preserve our prayer time. Unless we discipline ourselves and make a deliberate effort, little things will keep us from establishing a consistent devotional life. One of the Barnes' favorite mottos is: Say "no" to good things and save "yes" for the best. If we give God our squeezed-in or leftover part of our schedules, our quiet time will not be effective for growth.

Today's Action
- ◆ Start your "planned neglect" today.

Prayer
Father God, give me the discipline to say no to good things, so I can give first priority to You. Amen.

Ten Good Friends

❑
❑
❑

———————◇———————

"I wish that I had some good friends to help me on in life!" cried lazy Dennis.

"Good friends? Why, you have ten!" replied his master.

"I'm sure I haven't half so many; and those I have are too poor to help me."

"Count your fingers, my boy," said his master.

Dennis looked down at his strong hands.

"Count thumbs and all," added the master.

"I have; there are ten," said the lad.

"Then never say you have not ten good friends to help you on in life. Try what those true friends can do, before you go to grumbling and fretting because you do not get help from others."

—Source unknown

Many times we look to others to help us out, and we complain when we don't receive the help we think we deserve. Help starts within ourselves, then moves outward. We need to take an inventory of all the skills and tools God has so graciously given us at birth. We tend to take for granted those attributes of success that were given to us at the beginning of our lives—our fingers and thumbs!

Although we need to dig in and do our own work, sometimes we do need help. King Solomon, in all of his wisdom, tells us that friends are great blessings to our family. He emphasizes in Ecclesiastes 4:

- ◆ "Two are better than one because they have a good return for their labor" (verse 9).

- ◆ "Woe to the one who falls when there is not another to lift him up" (verse 10).

- ◆ "If two lie down together they keep warm" (verse 11).

- ◆ "If one can overpower him who is alone, two can resist him"(verse 12).

- ◆ "A cord of three strands is not quickly torn apart" (verse 12).

Are you working on relationships that build these blessings? Begin at home with your family members. Throughout Scripture we are told to be united with one another. Unity should be our goal: husband to wife, parent to child, child to sibling, friend to friend.

Begin to develop friends and traits that have eternal worth, not the temporal that last for only a short time.

Today's Action

- ◆ Evaluate your willingness to dig in and get the job done. Show your family and friends how much you appreciate them and their willingness to help.

Prayer

Father God, let me fully realize the gift of ten fingers that You have given me. I also want to thank You for the friends You've brought into my life.

Knowing God's Will

*Enter by the narrow gate; for the gate is wide,
and the way is broad that leads to destruction,
and many are those who enter by it. For the gate
is small, and the way is narrow that leads to life,
and few are those who find it.*

—Matthew 7:13,14

————◇————

How do we know God's will? Through the pages of His Word, the Bible. This is why it is important to read the Word of God every day. In the Bible are God's principles and directions for life—

- "I am not ashamed of the gospel, for it is the power of God for salvation to everyone who believes" (Romans 1:16).

- "Blessed is he who reads and those who hear the words of the prophecy, and heed the things which are written in it, for the time is near" (Revelation 1:3).

- "The unfolding of Thy words gives light; it gives understanding to the simple" (Psalm 119:130).

Today's Action
- Write down two decisions you need to make, then ask God for guidance.

Prayer
Father God, help me to have a discerning spirit when it comes to knowing Your plan for my life. Amen.

All Things New

Behold I am making all things new.

—Revelation 21:5

————◇————

As I get older and my body gets weaker I would certainly like to get a few new bones and muscles. Mine are getting tired and worn out. When my old buddies and I get together we have the war stories of all our new aches and pains.

For some of you, the desire for something new might revolve around a car that's wearing out, an old stove that needs replacing, a house that needs work, or maybe some plans and dreams that need renewal.

As believers in Christ we stand renewed because He is in the business of renewal. Jesus makes all things new. We are promised in 2 Corinthians 5:17, "If any man is in Christ, he is a new creature; the old things passed away; behold new things have come."

Give your needs and broken dreams to Jesus. He will renew you again and give you a newness to your spirit. Rise above your aches and pains, old cars, old appliances, and old homes. Approach Jesus in a brand-new way.

Today's Action

- ◆ Give Jesus your old nature and concerns, and watch Him turn them into something new. Stand in wonder and give the glory to God.

Prayer

Father God, I look forward with anticipation to see what You will make new in my life. Amen.

God Is with Us

Do not fear, for I am with you; do not anxiously
look about you, for I am your God.

—Isaiah 41:10

❏
❏
❏

———————◇———————

A few weeks ago it became evident that Emilie was having some physical problems. She did her best to mask over the warning signs, but there came a day when we realized that she had to go to the doctor. As she was examined, the doctor became quite concerned about the results of the blood test and a chest x-ray. With the findings in his hand, Dr. Merrihew said he was going to make an appointment for Emilie to see Dr. Ward, who is a well-known cancer specialist in our town. Needless to say that got our attention, and we were concerned about what he would find. Dr. Ward, after going through a battery of his own tests, recommended that Emilie come back for a bone-marrow scan that would tell us if any cancer cells were originating in the bone-marrow. Emilie asked for a four-week window in which to do this because we had a very busy speaking schedule that needed to be completed. Dr. Ward gave us this time because he felt Emilie's difficulties were chronic, not acute. All this time we, along with hundreds of friends, were praying that Emilie's body would return to normal. In the meantime she was taking a lot of nutritional foods that would raise the red blood cell count and lower the white blood cell count. Our four weeks were soon up, and we had a Tuesday morning appointment with Dr. Ward for another blood test and a bone-marrow scan.

A woman drew the blood and gave the test results to Dr. Ward. After reviewing the new data, he paused, looked at Emilie, and with a completely shocked expression asked, "What have you been doing?" Emilie very matter-of-factly replied, "Praying and eating good food supplements." Bottom line: No future treatment is expected (but we are to go back in for another blood test in three months). Today's Scripture was very real to us during this time of concern. Knowing that God is with us helped calm our concerns.

Today's Action

♦ Keep your eyes on God when you are in difficult times.

Prayer

Father God, let me fear not, knowing that You are with me and You will take care of my every need. Amen.

Self-discipline never means giving up anything, for giving up is a loss. Our Lord did not ask us to give up things of earth, but to exchange them for better things.

—*Fulton J. Sheen*

The Power of Silence

*But Jesus made no further answer; so that Pilate
was amazed.*

—Mark 15:5

————◇————

O h, if only I would have remained silent more often, but
I didn't. Through time, however, I'm learning that
silence is one of the greatest virtues of the Christian lifestyle.

A British writer, Mrs. Jessie Penn-Lewis, commenting on
the silences of Jesus, said that the Christian who is living close
to the Lord will manifest humility and self-control under the
most trying circumstances. Mrs. Lewis wrote:

> We will be silent in our lowly service among others,
> not seeking to be "seen of men." Silent while we
> stoop to serve the very ones who betrayed us. Silent
> when forced by others to some position where
> apparent rivalry with another much-abused servant
> of God seems imminent, only to be hushed by utter
> self-effacement in our silent withdrawal without
> explanation, irrespective of our "rights."

In our assertive generation, we seem to insist upon our
rights, and we argue to make people understand our position.
If we find ourselves having to verbally defend our actions,
then we may need to learn more from the silence of Jesus.

Today's Action

• Keep silent when you would like to answer back.

Prayer

*Father God, thank You for this reminder to keep silent because I
often want to set the record straight. Amen.*

Working for God

*Whatever you do, do your work heartily, as for
the Lord rather than for men.*

—Colossians 3:23

———◇———

oes your work seem like a waste of time? Consider your
office a place of ministry—then perform your duty as if
you're doing it for Jesus. *He's* the one you're really serving.

"Why do I do what I do? Is it to please man or God?"
These are two questions we must ask ourselves because how
we answer reveals how we look at life. If we work to please
people, we will never be satisfied because people always
expect more from us. If we work to please God, then we will
hop out of bed each morning to see what the new day brings.

We can profit by listening to John Dodd, who wrote several centuries ago: "Whatsoever our callings be, we serve the
Lord Christ in them....They are the most worthy servants...
that...serve the Lord, where He hath placed them."

If God's purposes are to be fulfilled, we must not neglect
the ordinary tasks in our pursuit of the glorious ones. Meals
must be cooked, trash must be collected, assembly lines must
be manned, and children must be attended to. *Every* service
done unto God is significant.

Today's Action

♦ Whatever God gives you to do, do it for Him.

Prayer

*Father God, help me think of my job as a ministry. May others
see Christ in my work. Amen.*

That's Business!

For we are His workmanship, created in Christ
Jesus for good works, which God prepared before-
hand, that we should walk in them.

—Ephesians 2:10

———◇———

The story is told about a man who claimed he "got reli-gion." An old crony who knew about his shameful past heard the news, called him on the phone, and said, "Joe, they tell me you've got religion."

"I sure have," came the reply.

His friend responded, "Then I suppose you'll be going to church every Sunday."

"That's right," Joe affirmed. "I started five weeks ago and haven't missed a service since."

"And I suppose you're going to quit smoking and drink-ing."

"Already have," Joe replied. "In fact, I haven't smoked a cigarette or touched a drop of liquor since."

His friend paused for a moment. Finally, remembering how much money Joe owed him, he said with an intended jab, "I suppose, too, that now you've got religion, you're going to pay all your old debts."

At that point Joe exploded and exclaimed, "Now wait a minute! That's not religion you're talking about; that's busi-ness!"

As a young college student, I made up my mind that I wanted to be more than just a Sunday Christian. I wanted my walk with the Lord to be a seven-day-a-week involvement. I figured that a religion that doesn't affect business wasn't worth much. Don't restrict God to certain rooms of your home; give Him the complete house. Unlock all the doors and give Him the keys. You'll find this is a much more rewarding lifestyle. The truth you tell on Sunday will be the same that you tell on Wednesday. Make sure that you walk your talk all week long.

Today's Action

◆ Does your religion also include your business?

Prayer

Father God, I do want to become an every-day Christian. Please give me strength daily. Amen.

Ordinary People

For who has despised the day of small things?

—Zechariah 4:10

❏
❏
❏

———◇———

We live in a day of comparisons. We look at homes, planes, boats, and cars to judge if ours are bigger or smaller than those around us. The world says we have to have the biggest. Small is not good. If we buy into this line of thought, we will spend our whole lives thinking we must work longer, smarter, and harder to improve our status in life.

When a small boy donated his two fishes and bread to Jesus, the Lord blessed his small lunch and it became a meal for many hungry people—and there was food to spare (see John 6:9-14). We must also depend on God's ability to take our smallness and use it for His glory. One of my favorite songs is "Ordinary People." It reflects on how God uses regular people to do His work. The Christian hall of fame is truly made up of men and women who were willing to serve Him in any way possible. Little is much if God is in it.

Today's Action

◆ Step forward today and volunteer for something that might seem small to the world.

Prayer

Father God, I pray that I might not despise small jobs. I realize that You are a God who will bless abundantly those things that seem insignificant to the world. Amen.

Authentic or Counterfeit

*For those who honor Me I will honor, and those
who despise Me will be lightly esteemed.*

—1 Samuel 2:30

A young man had just graduated from law school
and had set up an office, proudly displaying his
shingle out front. On his first day at work, as he sat
at his desk with his door open, he wondered how to
get his first client. Then he heard footsteps coming
down the long corridor toward his office.

Not wanting this potential client to think he would
be his first, he quickly picked up the telephone and
began to talk loudly to a make-believe caller.

"Oh, yes sir," the young lawyer exclaimed, "I'm
very experienced in corporate law... Courtroom
experience? Why, yes, I've had several cases."

The sound of steps drew closer to his open door.

"I have broad experience in almost every category
of legal work," he continued, loud enough for his
impending visitor to hear.

Finally, with the steps right at his door, he replied,
"Expensive? Oh, no sir, I'm very reasonable. I'm
told my rates are among the lowest in town."

The young lawyer then excused himself from his
"conversation" and covered the phone to respond
to the prospective client who was now standing in
the doorway. With his most confident voice he said,
"Yes, sir, may I help you?"

"Well, yes you can," the man said with a smirk. "I'm the telephone repairman, and I've come to hook up your phone!"

W e all sometimes fake the Christian life. Preoccupied with self and wanting our own way, we ignore God and pretend to be spiritual. Instead of having Christ's character imprinted on our lives, we go our own way, and our Christianity becomes a forgery. Like a counterfeit $100 bill, we may look real, but we lack genuine value.

Do you fake the Christian life? On Sunday, do you act and talk like a Christian, but come Monday or when you are away from church, do you forget all about your Christianity? If so, you are just like the young lawyer. You look good, talk good, and you act good, but your communication to God isn't right.

We feel best when our hearts are in good relationship to God. On the other hand, when we are disobedient to God we place a terrible yoke of guilt upon ourselves. On these occasions we feel like the counterfeit $100 bill—worthless.

Each day as we awake from our sleep we have two basic decisions to make:

- ◆ to obey God today
- ◆ to not obey God today

Today's Action

- ◆ Act in a way that reflects your authenticity. Be a true $100 bill.

Prayer

Father God, I want to be real in all aspects of my life. Amen.

What makes the temptation of power so seemingly irresistible? Maybe it is that power offers an easy substitute for the hard task of love. It seems easier to be God than to love God, easier to control people than to love people, easier to own life than to love life....

The long painful history of the church is the history of people ever and again tempted to choose power over love, control over the cross, being a leader over being led. Those who resisted this temptation to the end and thereby give us hope are the true saints.

—*Henri Nouwen*

Living Stones

You also, as living stones, are being built up as a spiritual house for a holy priesthood, to offer up spiritual sacrifices acceptable to God through Jesus Christ.

—1 Peter 2:5

———◇———

A man touring a rural area of the Far East saw a boy pulling a crude plow while an old man held the handles and guided it through the rice paddy. The visitor commented, "I suppose they are very poor."

"Yes," said his guide. "When their church was built, they wanted to give something to help but they had no money. So they sold their only ox."

In America we may not have to give up an ox and pull the plow ourselves, but there are many ways we can give. I am always amazed when I go out to a job site and see pallet after pallet of bricks and stones. They're just sitting there, not much beauty to them at all. But when I go back in a few weeks, I'm startled by what the skilled mason has done with those stones. They have become fireplaces, ornamental decorations for homes, retaining walls, and walkways.

God wants to make a "spiritual house" from all of our "living stones." Some spiritual sacrifices for the transformation will be costly, but what is gained by our giving—God's praise—is always greater than what we give.

Today's Action

◆ Let God use you to build a strong spiritual home.

Prayer

Father God, it's amazing what You can do with a pile of stones! Amen.

Strength's Weakness

*But Peter said to Him, "Even though all may
fall away, yet I will not."*

—Mark 14:29

———◇———

"Mother," said little Nezzie one morning after having
fallen from the bed, "I think I know why I fell out of
bed last night. It was because I slept too near the place where
I got in." Thinking a little more he added, "No, that was not
the reason; it was because I slept too near where I fell out."

How often we think that we can pass a test that others
have failed. Youngsters especially are so confident of their
strength. When I need some "grunt work" done around the
house I love to hire some over-confident youths who think
they can lift a piano all by themselves. The heavier the object,
the more assured they are. Give them a positive comment
about their strength, and they just beam with delight.

Unfortunately, many times in our strength we become
weak and our barriers against temptation fall one by one. We
discover we are not so immune to the snare of sin after all.
Peter, who loved Jesus with great passion, fell by that very
passion. "Not I, Master," he said. "Yes, Peter, even you!" the
Lord replied.

Yes, Lord I will fall unless I trust to your mercy and goodness to keep me safe.

Today's Action
♦ Read and meditate on 1 Corinthians 10:12.

Prayer
*Father God, help me remember that I am capable of falling. I
know I must continually be on guard. Amen.*

An Outcast's Love

*But a certain Samaritan, who was on a journey,
came upon him; and when he saw him, he felt
compassion.*

—Luke 10:33

❏
❏
❏

---◇---

The Samaritans were descendants of colonists whom the Assyrian kings planted in Palestine after the fall of the northern kingdom in 721 B.C. They were despised by the Jews because of their mixed Gentile and Jewish blood and their worship, which centered on Mt. Gerizim. On this mountain the Samaritans had built a temple to rival the one in Jerusalem, from which they had long been separated politically and religiously.

In this segment of Scripture, Luke 10:30-37, two other travelers had passed by, even the priest. But the one whose name wasn't even worthy of mentioning, the one regarded as alien and foreign, he is the one who bandaged the victim's wounds, took him to an inn, fed him, and rented a room for him until he recovered.

This certainly reflects genuine love, for the Samaritan didn't even know the man. Maybe the Samaritan, an outcast, understood the pain of neglect and rejection and so ministered to this man in need. Let us follow his example.

Today's Action
* ◆ Perform a "good Samaritan" act today.

Prayer
Father God, I need to be more compassionate to those in need. Help me in this deficiency. Amen.

The Gentle Comforter

And He shall wipe away every tear from their eyes; and there shall no longer be any death; there shall no longer be any mourning, or crying, or pain....

—Revelation 21:4

———◇———

The other day Emilie and I received a very early morning telephone call from my cousin in Texas. She told us with deep sobs that her 95-year-old mother (my aunt) had passed away during the night. Her sorrow was so very evident that she could hardly speak clearly. My aunt's death was especially hard to bear because she was my mother's only living sibling (of an original 13). After hanging up on the phone, today's verse of Scripture came to me. God shall gently brush away our tears with His comforts of empathy and sorrow, for He is the Father of mercies.

His promise is that He *shall* (*not* that He might) erase the grief that grips our minds and hearts. All of life's miseries that cause our hearts to mourn will be cast in a dark hole never to appear again.

Today's Action

- ◆ Know that someday all of your tears will be wiped away.

Prayer

Father God, as I grieve today, I will look forward to the day when there will be no sorrow, pain, or mourning. Amen.

The Greatest Motive

Walk in a manner worthy of the Lord, to please Him in all respects.

—Colossians 1:10

❑
❑
❑
❑

———◇———

A first-grader beamed with satisfaction as he handed his parents a spelling test on which his teacher had written a large "100—Good Work!" The boy later said, "I showed this to Dad and Mom because I knew it would please them." I can just see him riding home on the bus, hardly able to wait for the moment when his parents would express their excitement with how well he had done.

A strong desire to please God is the highest incentive we have for doing His will. We may have other worthy motives, such as the inner satisfaction gained from doing what's right or the anticipation of receiving rewards in heaven, but we bring the greatest glory to God when we obey and serve Him because we long to do what brings Him delight.

I was an excellent student because I had a burning desire to please the teachers. I did my homework on time and raised my hand before I spoke. This led to great satisfaction when my teacher would write on my paper, "100—Good Work!"

Many times Jesus put His own desires aside and chose to please God. Jesus prayed, "Not My will, but Thine be done." His greatest motive was His desire to please His Father. That is quite an incentive for us too.

Today's Action

◆ Do something to honor God.

Prayer

Father God, may I be a God-pleaser more than a people-pleaser. Amen.

For God to explain a trial would be to destroy its object, which is that of calling forth simple faith and implicit obedience.

—*Alfred Edersheim*

Belling the Cat

Be strong and courageous! Do not tremble or be dismayed, for the LORD your God is with you wherever you go.

—Joshua 1:9

———◇———

Once upon a time all the mice met together in council to discuss the best means of protecting themselves against the attacks of the cat. After several suggestions had been debated, a mouse of some standing and experience got up and said, "I think I have hit upon a plan which ensures our safety in the future, provided you approve and carry it out. It is that we should fasten a bell around the neck of our enemy the cat, which will by its tinkling warn us of her approach."

This proposal was warmly applauded, and they had decided to adopt it, when an old mouse finally got up. He said, "I agree with you all that the plan before us is an admirable one; but, I ask, who is going to bell the cat?"

—Adapted from *The Mice in a Meeting*, an Aesop fable

Wouldn't it be wonderful if all we had to do in order to be brave is talk about it? But true courage and bravery require action. Our society hungers to find people with courage. We look for our heroes in sports, politics, movies, and business and church leaders—many of them fail the test. We long for the character trait of courage, but few people are able to deliver it.

As parents we are continually tested by the decisions we must make. Are we able to stand alone and make hard decisions regarding what we as a family are going to do? It's hard to be in the minority as a friend, a neighbor, a parent, or a Christian and just say no.

In Joshua 24:15 the writer has a similar dilemma, but he stood tall and delivered this statement:

> If it is disagreeable in your sight to serve the LORD, choose for yourselves today whom you will serve: whether the gods which your fathers served which were beyond the River, or the gods of the Amorites in whose land you are living; but as for me and my house, we will serve the LORD.

Joshua was willing to stand up and be heard. He had the courage to place the bell on the cat. Are you facing a similar difficulty in your life? If so, look to God to find the answer. He says that He will never leave us or forsake us (Hebrews 13:5). That is a promise we can take to the bank.

Emilie and I have some friends in northern California who have made a "valor ribbon" for each of their two sons. When the parents are aware that the sons have taken some action that requires courage, bravery, or valor they recognize that by letting the boys wear their ribbons that evening at home. It might be for:

- not smoking, drinking, or taking drugs when someone offers them
- not cheating on a test when the opportunity arises
- saying no to premarital sex
- returning found money
- assisting someone who is in need of help

These parents recognize the importance of praising their sons' acts of courage.

Today's Action

- In what areas of your life do you need to show more courage? What are you going to do about it?

Prayer

Father God, I want to have enough courage to stand up and be counted in difficult situations. Let me be able to bell the cat. Amen.

The Pursuit of Godliness

With a long life I will satisfy him, and let him behold My salvation.

—Psalm 91:16

❑
❑
❑

———◇———

In America we are going through major changes in our health and medical insurance programs. The medical profession itself is not what it used to be because major changes have been made and more are to come. Healthcare is a major political issue: How are we going to take care of the sick, and who will pay for these services?

The Bible associates health, prosperity, and longevity with godliness. Psalm 91 is filled with assurances of God's love and provision. In verse 16 God declares that He will deliver, protect, honor, and give long life to the one who trusts Him. It is well-known in the medical profession that an amazingly large percentage of human disease and suffering is directly traceable to worry, fear, conflict, immorality, dissipation—unwholesome thinking and unclean living. If people would pursue godly lives much of the illnesses we find in America and throughout the world would be wiped out.

Godliness *does* lead to blessing—even during dark times. If we place our trust in God, we can look for His favor in our lives.

Today's Action

♦ God says He will give us a long life if we strive for godliness. How are you going to use your days?

Prayer

Father God, even during my dark times I thank You for Your abundant promises. I look forward to a long life. Amen.

The Purpose of Suffering

And after you have suffered for a little while, the God of all grace, who called you to His eternal glory in Christ, will Himself perfect, confirm, strengthen and establish you.

—1 Peter 5:10

———————◇———————

Wouldn't it be wonderful to grow into full Christian maturity without having to suffer? I've talked to many godly senior citizens—both men and women—and I'm amazed at the events that have made them into such dedicated people of God.

These friends have shared the pain they have experienced along the way that helped mold them into Christlike beings. Oh, yes, they have had their times of exuberance, but they didn't seem to build the inner character that Peter is talking about in today's verse. Peter wanted to give a message of encouragement to those scattered throughout the Roman Empire because he knew there would be a lot of suffering inflicted by the then pagan society. He said, don't count the hard times as lost, but rejoice because after a while God Himself will perfect (make you mature), confirm, strengthen, and establish you. These are attributes of my senior citizen friends. So when we are suffering, know that God is molding us, helping us become like Christ. Count it all joy.

Today's Action

- ◆ How is God using today's circumstances to help you mature in your walk with Jesus?

Prayer

Father God, I look forward to the good work You'll do in my life. Mold me and shape me as You will. Amen.

Setting Boundaries

A joyful heart makes a cheerful face, but when
the heart is sad, the spirit is broken.

—Proverbs 15:13

❏
❏
❏

————◇————

P arenting is an overwhelming task, and how to discipline our children is one of the most perplexing aspects of the job. We often feel we are in a tug-of-war with our children. The natural tendency is to throw in the towel and give up (that's what the children hope for). Far too often I've seen parents who have given up this task of gently yet firmly shaping their children's will. Children who battle the loving authority of their parents are greatly reassured when the response is consistent, firm, and confident. They find their greatest security in a structural environment where the rights of other people are protected by defined boundaries. It takes godly wisdom to provide this kind of security.

One of the main purposes of discipline in our home was to have our children realize that they were responsible for their actions and accountable for their behavior. One of the goals of parents is to provide children with solid direction and self-assurance that will see them through life. I encourage you to read the book of Proverbs. It contains some specific verses that offer good biblical principles for raising children.

Today's Action
- ◆ Do you and your spouse have a clear direction regarding your children's discipline? If not, spend time together to define these areas.

Prayer
Father God, grant me the wisdom to use proper discipline with my children. Amen.

Winning the Race

*Let endurance have its perfect result, that you
may be perfect and complete, lacking in nothing.*

—James 1:4

A hare was one day making fun of a tortoise for
being so slow on his feet.

"Wait a bit," said the tortoise. "I'll run a race with
you, and I'll wager that I win."

"Oh, well," replied the hare, who was much
amused at the idea. "Let's try and see."

It was soon agreed that the fox should set a course
for them and be the judge. When the time came
both started off together, but the hare was soon so
far ahead he thought he might as well have a rest;
so down he lay and fell fast asleep. Meanwhile the
tortoise kept plodding on and reached the goal. At
last the hare woke up with a start and dashed to the
finish line, only to find that the tortoise had already
won the race.

—An Aesop fable

Too many of us only see the start of the race. So much of
life is painted with speed, flash, and sizzle that we can be
intimidated.

A few years ago my family went to Lake Tahoe to ski during the Christmas break. As I walked on the icy slopes of this
beautiful resort my eyes were full of the best—the best cars,
skis, clothes, and beauty. I couldn't believe my eyes; I had
never seen so much sizzle in one place.

So I said to myself, "No way am I going to compete with
them." After being coaxed into my group ski lesson I found

that members of the sizzle group were also in my class, and they couldn't ski any better than I could!

Today's Scripture teaches that perseverance is enduring with patience. In the Bible, perseverance describes Christians who faithfully endure and remain steadfast in the face of opposition, attack, and discouragement. When we persevere with patience, we exhibit our ability to endure with calmness and without complaint. As believers we must daily commit ourselves to godly living.

Commitment and discipline are not words that the world is comfortable with. The 90s decade wants everything to feel good—but perseverance doesn't always feel good. It sometimes demands denial of self and pain. That's why trusting and having faith in God's guidance is so important.

Scripture is clear when it teaches we are to persevere—

- ◆ in prayer (Ephesians 6:18)
- ◆ in obedience (Revelation 14:12)
- ◆ in self-control (2 Peter 1:5-7)

Scripture promises us certain blessings if we endure:

- ◆ final deliverance (Matthew 24:13)
- ◆ rewarded faith (Hebrews 11:6)
- ◆ eternal inheritance (Revelation 21:7)

As we live out our lives and persevere daily against all the trials and temptations, we are rewarded by the Lord with the fruit of His Spirit for all eternity (see Galatians 5:22,23):

◆ love	◆ goodness	◆ patience
◆ joy	◆ faithfulness	◆ kindness
◆ peace	◆ gentleness	◆ self-control

Today's Action

- ◆ Jot down several struggles you are having in life. Beside each one list several things that God is trying to teach you through them.

Prayer

Father God, in life's difficulties help me look to You to see what You are trying to teach me. Amen.

What the majority of American children needs is to stop being pampered, stop being indulged, stop being chauffeured, stop being catered to. In the final analysis, it is not what you do for children but what you taught them to do for themselves that will make them successful human beings.

—Ann Landers

Jonathan and David

> *Now it came about when he had finished speaking to Saul, that the soul of Jonathan was knit to the soul of David, and Jonathan loved him as himself.*

—1 Samuel 18:1

———◇———

Samuel Johnson wrote, "We cannot tell the precise moment when friendship is formed. As in filling a vessel drop by drop, there is at last a drop which makes it run over; so in a series of kindness there is at last one which makes the heart run over."

In 1 Samuel 18, 19, and 23 we discover one of the finest examples of friendship—the deep relationship between Jonathan, the king's son, and David, a shepherd boy. They accepted each other even though socially they were far apart. They depended on each other's strengths to shore up their individual weaknesses. David and Jonathan exhibited several traits that are found in friendships:

- unconditional love
- personal enjoyment
- mutual acceptance
- mutual interests
- mutual commitment
- mutual loyalty

To be a friend you must be involved in the other person's life—it takes time and commitment to be a friend. You have to be willing to put your friend's needs above your own.

Today's Action

- Take inventory of who your real friends are. Give them a call and let them know they're important to you.

Prayer

Father God, thank You for my friends who love me. Amen.

Teaching by Example

I exhort you, therefore, be imitators of me.

—1 Corinthians 4:16

◇

One night when a father was praying with his son, the boy asked a very penetrating question.

"Dad, have I ever met a Christian?"

The father was taken aback, realizing that his son had not caught what he was attempting to teach the lad.

Are you living for Christ in a way that you are modeling Christ to your children?

In bygone days a father who was a skilled tradesman would take on his son as an apprentice. This required many years of training so the apprentice could qualify as a journeyman. This was teaching by example. There are very few trades that are taught like that anymore; vocations have become far too complex.

However, in the family setting children still learn by example. They learn by seeing mom and dad in action. They see their parents' values and ethics put into practice.

Your "little apprentices" are watching everything you do in the car, at a ball game, in church, around the meal table—everywhere! These are great opportunities to teach your children the important values of life. Children's eyes are always open to example.

Today's Action

- ◆ Spend quality time with your children today. Let them see and hear you make godly decisions.

Prayer

Father God, thanks for the reminder that my children are looking to me to help them become adults. Amen.

Listening to God's Questions

The LORD answered Job, "Who is this that dark-
ens counsel by words without knowledge?"

—Job 38:2

❑
❑
❑
❑

———◇———

God literally answered Job's question by asking him a question. How absurd to think that a creature should become the critic of the Creator!

Two of my mom's favorite television programs are "Jeopardy" and "Wheel of Fortune." They ask question after question. Some of the contestants are so knowledgeable and quick that the others get left behind.

We are fascinated by questions. I often run into people who say, "When I get to heaven I'm going to ask God why He did this and why He did that." I just sit back knowing that if we met God face-to-face we would be in so much awe that we would know that our questions would be very trivial in the presence of His majesty.

In the book of Job there are 288 questions asked. Seventy-eight of them are God's responses to Job's questions.

As men, let's be keenly aware when God is asking us penetrating questions that truly require us to reveal who we are—humbled, awed, speechless, weak, and believing.

Today's Action

◆ Let each of God's questions bring you closer to Him. Examine today a question that He has been asking you. What answer is required?

Prayer

Father God, let me come to You with knowledge that reflects my awe of You. Amen.

Working in Unity

For even as the body is one and yet has many members, and all the members of the body, though they are many, are one body, so also is Christ.

—1 Corinthians 12:12

———◇———

In this verse Paul describes the relationship between believers by using the analogy of the human body. The Holy Spirit has formed a spiritual unit from the many dissimilar members of the body of Christ (1 Corinthians 12,13). The workability of the human body and the body of Christ demands that *all* members function in oneness. In 1 Corinthians 12:21-31, we observe the need for mutual dependence, respect, and care.

Recently Emilie experienced a loss of energy. Her sinuses were plugging up, and she had low endurance. In going to the doctor for a check-up, the blood test indicated that Emilie's white cell blood count was too high, and her red cell blood count was too low. Not until she brought these levels back into balance was she able to function properly. For the human body to function properly all parts must work together.

That's the way it is in our "body life." In order to be healthy, all members must function together in unity. Great churches have many members properly using their gifts to make the body of Christ whole.

Today's Action

♦ Notice where your church body needs help and reach out. Begin to serve with your gifts.

Prayer

Father God, I appreciate You letting me use my gifts. Amen.

The Decision to Love

*Love is patient, love is kind, and is not jealous;
love does not brag and is not arrogant, [it] does
not act unbecomingly; it does not seek its own,
is not provoked, does not take into account a
wrong suffered, does not rejoice in unrighteousness, but rejoices with the truth; bears all
things, believes all things, hopes all things,
endures all things. Love never fails....*

—Corinthians 13:4-8

O ne of the most searching questions we have to answer
as adults is "What is love?" We see people who search
so hard yet miss the mark; they aren't able to grasp love in
either their heads or their hearts.

The people of the '90s seem so dysfunctional when it
comes to the topic of love. What we read, hear, and watch
seems to fall short of what true love really is. As young babies,
we enter the world with much love bestowed on us by our
parents and grandparents. Although they make such a fuss
over us and give us so much attention, somewhere along the
line we seemed to lose grasp of the concept of committing to
love no matter what. Through the years we've gone from a
decision to love to a *feeling* of love. We have lost our focus.
Some confusing signals we get regarding love are that:

- we fall in and out of love
- love is a feeling too deep for words
- love means never having to say you're sorry
- we can give it a trial run
- love is a sickness full of woes
- love is a warm puppy

No wonder we're confused when we get real serious about
true love! The Greeks had three levels of love:

- *Agape:* love for an adorable object
- *Eros:* physical love between husband and wife
- *Phileo:* brotherly love for others

Our western culture tries to describe all these relationships with one encompassing word: *love.* This doesn't let us define the degrees or types of love.

When Paul wrote to the church in Corinth he told them to come together in love rather than in chaos and disharmony. Paul contrasted the present with what Christ would be like in heaven. He showed the supremacy of love over conflicts.

If we could only recapture this agape love that Paul spoke about, we could become healthy, wholesome, and functional families again. My cry is that love is much more than a warm puppy. It is an unselfish decision to love and honor your commitment to another person and to God.

Today's Action

- Show your wife that your love is based on commitment and not on feeling.

Prayer

Father God, I sometimes get confused between decision and feeling. Thank You for today's reminder. Amen.

The men who have pride and peace of mind
And the respect of other men ...
The men who say in their twilight years
That they'd do it all again ...
The men who love the flowers and trees
And watching the animals play ...
These are wealthy men, for what they have
Can never be taken away.

—*George E. Young*

Where Is Your Joy?

These things I have spoken to you, that My joy may be in you, and that your joy may be made full.

—John 15:11

————◇————

Sometimes after we meet people in church we walk away thinking, "Where is their joy? If they had it, they certainly have lost it." In today's verse we see that Jesus has given us abundant joy. He gave us a *fullness* of joy—and that's a lot. Do members of your family consider you a joyful person? If you asked them this question what would they say? I encourage you to ask them. I can remember one of my Sunday school teachers writing on the chalkboard:

Jesus
O
You

This illustrates that there is nothing between Jesus and you—and that's the gospel truth. In order to have joy all we need is Jesus and ourselves—nothing more, nothing less.

Today's Action
* ◆ Read these verses to help you with the joy idea: Psalm 104:34, Luke 10:20, Acts 2:28.

Prayer
Father God, thank You for Your radiance. Life would be gloomy without Your influence on my life. Amen.

Bombarded by Confusion

Come, my people, enter into your rooms, and
close your doors behind you; hide for a little
while.

—**Isaiah 26:20**

───────◇───────

These days there is a restlessness and a fearfulness that stand like two granite walls against godliness. Wherever one turns there is an air of confusion and loud noises. MTV is a clear reflection of today's restlessness. If you go to a restaurant, you will observe children who can't sit quietly in their chairs for more than five minutes. Action, action, action—every place one looks there is action.

Oh, the joy of tranquillity! How our hearts yearn for quietness! But we are bombarded with rock music, loud ads, and nerve-crackling television programs with their senseless laugh tracks.

What can we do to find peacefulness? Why is serenity so important? Scripture gives us guidance and encouragement in this area:

- ◆ Paul tells us to pray for those in authority so that we can lead tranquil and quiet lives (1 Timothy 2:1,2).

- ◆ We are guaranteed that in quietness and trust we have our strength (Isaiah 30:15).

- ◆ God is the author of peace, not confusion (1 Corinthians 14:33).

Today's Action
- ◆ Turn off all loud noises. Close the doors behind you. Experience peace in the presence of God.

Prayer
Father God, create in me a quiet spirit. Amen.

Why Didn't He Run?

Be subject to one another in the fear of Christ.

—Ephesians 5:21

❑
❑
❑

—————◇—————

You've probably never heard of Nicolai Pestretsov, but now you may never forget him. He was 36 years old, a sergeant major in the Russian army, stationed in Angola. His wife had traveled the long distance from home to visit him when, on an August day, South African military units entered the country in quest of black nationalist guerrillas taking sanctuary there. When the South Africans encountered the Russian soldiers, four people were killed and the rest of the Russians fled—except for Sergeant Major Pestretsov.

The South African troops captured Pestretsov, and a military communiqué explained the situation: "Sergeant Major Nicolai Pestretsov refused to leave the body of his slain wife, who was killed in the assault on the village. He went to the body of his wife and would not leave it, although she was dead."

What a picture of commitment—and what a series of questions it raises! Robert Fulghum, in *All I Really Know I Learned in Kindergarten,* tells this story, then asks these questions:

> Why didn't he run and save his own hide? What made him go back? Is it possible that he loved her? Is it possible that he wanted to hold her in his arms one last time? Is it possible that he needed to cry and grieve? Is it possible that he felt the stupidity of war? Is it possible that he felt the injustice of fate? Is it possible that he didn't care what became of him now? Is it possible? We don't know. Or at least we don't know for certain. But we can guess. His actions answer.

What do your actions say about your commitment to your wife? What do your attitudes and your words reveal? Standing by the commitment you made to your spouse—the commitment you made before God and witnesses—is key to standing by your wife.

Today's Action

◆ Today in your journal write down a fresh, new commitment to God and to your spouse.

Prayer

Father God, help me stay true to the marriage vow I made before You and other witnesses. Amen.

Now Is the Time!

> *But as for me and my house, we will serve the Lord.*
>
> **—Joshua 24:15**

———◇———

Your life today is the result of the decisions you made yesterday. Unfortunately, we all make bad decisions sometimes. Are you tired of being a slave to poor decisions of the past? If so, you can have the freedom and joy of being in Christ. Paul writes in Romans 10:9,10, "If you confess with your mouth Jesus as Lord, and believe in your heart that God raised Him from the dead, you shall be saved; for with the heart man believes, resulting in righteousness, and with the mouth he confesses, resulting in salvation."

Can you make a decision today affirming this promise? It will be the best decision of your life. Don't delay. The writer of Ecclesiastes 3:1 states, "There is a time for everything, and a season for every activity" (NIV).

Three times a soldier picked up the hymn "Will You Go?" which was scattered as a tract. Twice he threw it down. The last time he read it, he took his pencil and wrote, "By the grace of God, I will try to go, John Waugh, Company G, Tenth Regiment, P.R.V.C." That night he went to a prayer meeting, read his resolution, and requested prayer for his salvation. He said, "I am not ashamed of Christ; but I am ashamed of myself for having been so long ashamed of him." He was killed a few months later. How timely was his resolution!

Today's Action

- ◆ Today is the appointed time. Make a decision for Christ or reconfirm that you will serve the Lord.

Prayer

Father God, I want to serve You with all my heart and soul. Please renew that desire in me daily. Amen.

Has the Label Changed?

Encourage one another day after day. . .lest any one of you be hardened by the deceitfulness of sin.

—Hebrews 3:13

———◇———

We live in an age when people change labels if the name is "too harsh." The word *sin* is too negative, so many people hedge and call it everything but what it is. And people don't want to feel convicted or guilty when they leave church; they want to feel comfortable. Consequently, they harden their hearts and are deceived when sin creeps up on them.

Popular evangelist Wilbur Chapman told of a friend who delivered a powerful sermon on the subject of sin. After the service, one of the church officers confronted the minister and offered what he thought was needed counsel: "Pastor, we don't want you to talk as openly as you do about man's guilt and corruption. If our boys and girls hear you discussing that subject they will more easily become sinners. Call it a mistake, if you will, but do not speak so plainly about sin."

The pastor took out a small bottle.

Showing it to the man, he said, "See this label? It says 'Strychnine' and underneath in bold, red letters is the word 'poison.' What you are asking me to do would be like changing this label to 'Essence of Peppermint.' Someone who doesn't know the danger might use it and become very ill."

What an important reminder! Stay alert and be sensitive to what sin is—don't accept any other label. It is vital that we confess and forsake sin, but we can do that only when we use the right label.

Today's Action

♦ Examine your life to see if you've relabeled any sin. Confess it and get back on track.

Prayer

Father God, let me not harden my heart to what sin is. Amen.

247

It is painful, being a man, to have to assert the privilege, or the burden, which Christianity lays upon my own sex. I am crushingly aware of how inadequate most of us are, in our actual and historical individualities, to fill the place prepared for us.

—*C.S. Lewis*

"Can't You Say It, Dad?"

Behold, children are a gift of the LORD.

—**Psalm 127:3**

———◇———

O h look, Daddy, I catched it!"

"That's my boy. Now get ready; here comes another. Make me proud and catch this one too."

"Look, Daddy, I'm only eight years old and I can throw faster than anyone in the league!"

"But your batting stinks, Tiger. Can't play in the big leagues if you can't hit."

"Look, Dad, I'm 16 and I've already made the varsity team!"

"You'd better do a little less bragging and a little more practicing on your defense. Still needs a lot of work."

"Look, Father, I'm 35 and the company has made me a vice president!"

"Maybe someday you'll start your own business like your old man, then you'll really feel a sense of accomplishment."

"Look at me, Dad, I'm 40, successful, well-respected in the community. I have a wonderful wife and family—aren't you proud of me now, Dad?

"All my life it seems I've caught everything but that one prize I wanted most—your approval. Can't you say it, Dad? Is it too much to ask for? Just once I'd like to know that feeling every child should have of being loved unconditionally. I'd like for you to put your arm around my shoulders and, instead of telling me I'm not good enough, tell me that in your eyes I'm already a winner and always will be no matter what.

"Look at me, Daddy, I'm all grown up . . . but in my heart still lives a little boy who yearns for his father's love. Won't you pitch me the words I've waited for all my life?

"I'll catch them, Father, I promise."

Do your children know you love them? Do your children know unconditional acceptance? Are they winners in your eyes? Do they know that? Children need to know that mom and dad really love them. They long to hear us say, "I love you, and I am very proud of you." And they need to know we love them even when they . . .

- ◆ yell and scream in the grocery store
- ◆ have temper tantrums in a restaurant
- ◆ wear strange clothes
- ◆ have funny haircuts and oddly colored hair
- ◆ use vulgar language
- ◆ run away from home
- ◆ do poorly in school
- ◆ run around with "questionable" friends

Often children use behaviors such as these to ask, "Do you love me always?" What are your children hearing from your reaction?

Today's Action

- ◆ Write each of your children—whatever their ages—a note to let them know how much you love them. Be specific about a few things you love about them.

Prayer

Father God, teach me to show my children that I love them and prod me to tell them with words, too. Amen.

Knocking Down the Walls

For He Himself is our peace, who made both groups into one, and broke down the barrier of the dividing wall.

—Ephesians 2:14

———◇———

It was agreed upon by the armies of the Romans and the Albans to put the trial of all to the issue of a battle between six brothers; three on the one side, the sons of Curatius; and three on the other, the sons of Horatius. While the Curatiuses were united, though all three sorely wounded, they killed two of the Horatiuses. The third began to take to his heels, though not hurt at all, but when he saw them follow slowly, the distance between each brother increasing because of wounds and heavy armor, he fell upon them one after another, and slew all three.

It is the cunning sleight of the devil to divide us, that he may prevail against us. This is the end result of division regardless of where we find it.

Wouldn't it be wonderful if warring spouses, siblings, coworkers, church members—all who have battles going on within hurting hearts—would come together before God? He is peace, and He longs to destroy the barriers of misunderstanding and hatred. God *can heal* the rift between two or more parties. His love can be the glue that repairs broken relations, putting them back together again. Step out in faith and ask Him to intervene if you are in the midst of conflict.

Today's Action

- Step out today. Let God heal that broken relationship. Let His love flow through you.

Prayer

Father God, may I be the vehicle You use to knock down walls that divide. Amen.

The Heart of Unity

*For this cause a man shall leave his father and
his mother, and shall cleave to his wife; and they
shall become one flesh.*

—Genesis 2:23

————◇————

If we don't stand together as husband and wife, letting God
make us one in spite of our differences, we will easily be
defeated. That is one reason why God calls a couple to:

- ◆ departure ("a man will leave his father and mother")
- ◆ permanence ("and cleave to his wife")
- ◆ oneness ("they shall become one flesh")

Becoming one doesn't mean becoming the same.
However, oneness means sharing the same degree of commitment to the Lord and to the marriage, the same goals and
dreams, and the same mission in life. It's an internal conformity to one another, not an external conformity. Oneness
results when two individuals reflect the same Christ. Such
spiritual unity produces tremendous strength in a marriage
and in a family.

For this togetherness to happen, the two marriage partners
must leave their families (mom and dad) and let God make
them one. We men help the cleaving process when we show—
not just tell—our wives that they are our most important priorities after God.

If you clearly communicate your love to your wife, your
marriage relationship will become more dynamic.

Today's Action

- ◆ Show and tell your wife that you love her in a way you
  don't usually do.

Prayer

*Father God, show me how to help work with my wife to bring
unity in purpose and spirit to our marriage. Amen.*

Choosing Silence

Cease striving [be still] and know that I am God.

—Psalm 46:10

❏
❏
❏

---◇---

Have you ever gone outside on a cold, snowy morning before the animals and birds have put their tracks in the freshly fallen snow? What an exuberance that creates in the heart. It is so very quiet, with not a sound being echoed. This is what I envision stillness to be. Such a contrast to the freeway, airport, and other noises we are bombarded with—the blare of the stereo, the TV, the children, and the arguments.

Habakkuk 2:20 tells us, "The LORD is in His holy temple. Let all the earth be silent before Him." Experiencing this silence isn't a choice—it's more like a command. If we aren't silent by our own choosing, there will be a time and place when our physical bodies will give out because of all the stimulation; we will lie sleepless because of illness, heartache, grief, or anxiety. In those moments of quietness we can learn lessons we chose not to learn on our own. Don't wait until the silence is cast upon you. Practice daily stillness and silence.

Today's Action
- Set aside time to be silent before God.

Prayer
Father God, I'm committed to developing a daily time of quietness—just me and You. Amen.

Marriage

Perhaps the greatest blessing in marriage is that it lasts so long. The years, like the varying interests of each other.... In a series of temporary relationships, one misses the ripening, gathering, harvesting joys, the deep, hard-won truths of marriage.

—*Richard C. Cabot*

Keeping on Track

My righteous one shall live by faith; and if he shrinks back, My soul has no pleasure in him.

—Hebrews 10:38

————◇————

E milie and I recently attended a 30-year reunion of some couples who were instrumental in founding a great church in Newport Beach, California. As we looked at old photo albums and colored slides, we were awestruck by our youthfulness during this period of our walk with the Lord. We laughed, we cried, we hugged, we ate, and we recalled ups and downs, joys and sorrows, births and deaths. We marveled that over the years we had all remained faithful to God's calling, and all of us were still involved in God's work in our local ministries—even though most of us had moved away.

We persevered in our faith. We did not let obstacles and disappointments divert us from our paths. We continued to grow and mature in the Lord. In 2 Timothy 3:14 Paul tells Timothy, "Continue in the things you have learned." This was Paul's way of encouraging this young man to, "keep on track."

We all have setbacks, but we need to persevere. If you find yourself disappointed today, I encourage you to continue in the things you have learned.

Today's Action

♦ Keep on keeping on.

Prayer

Father God, may I not be a quitter in my life; I want to be victorious even to the end. Amen.

Red Lights Mean Stop!

Oh that my ways may be established to keep Thy statutes!

—Psalm 119:5

————◇————

salm 119 conveys the truth that the Word of God contains everything man needs to know. If you live in a mid-to large-size city you know the trick of trying to time your driving to hit all the green lights on your most traveled route. You can really get good because you've got it down pat. You almost yell with exuberance, "I did it, I didn't have to stop once!" However, when that occasional miscalculation occurs and you come to one of those big yellow lights you have a decision to make: Do you risk going through a late yellow light or do you stop?

Most of us don't like red lights in our lives, but they serve a valuable purpose. In traffic they prevent accidents; in life God puts them there as prohibitions against selfishness, envy, hatred, lust, pride, and irreverence. When these personal red lights flash we need to stop immediately. If we run the lights we are really heading for trouble.

Be as respectful of God's red lights as you are of city statutes. He is trying to teach you something.

Today's Action

◆ Be ready to stop at God's red lights.

Prayer

Father God, help me anticipate and recognize any red lights that are ahead of me. Amen.

Creator or Created?

*Thus says the LORD "I am the first and I am the
last, and there is no God besides me."*

—Isaiah 44:6

❑
❑
❑

———◇———

As men we struggle with who will be our God. Will it be
a person, a job, more wealth, a possession, or will it be
the almighty God? Idolatry is placing our longings for what
only God can provide in the hands of a created creature
instead of the Creator. When we base our lives on false gods
created by man, instead of depending on God the Creator, we
will eventually realize that life doesn't have meaning and is
void of fulfillment. The writers of Scripture are quite clear that
dependency on a false god will result in loss, pain, and shame
(Isaiah 42:17; 44:9-11). A false god will leave emptiness and
disappointment.

We need to continually evaluate our lives to see why we
do what we do. What is our motivation? Are we trying to
please the Creator or the created? If we are honest with ourselves we can change course and go in another direction. It's
important that we let God work in our lives. We need to be as
soft as new clay so we can be remolded. If we become hard, we
become brittle and fragile. We need to keep our eyes on the
Lord, so He will direct our paths.

Today's Action

♦ Look in the mirror. Who do you see—the Creator or the
created?

Prayer

Father God, restore my vision so I see only You. Amen.

How Can We Give Thanks?

*In everything give thanks; for this is God's will
for you in Christ Jesus.*

—1 Thessalonians 5:18

———◇———

This is one of the most difficult passages for us to understand. How do we say "Thank You, God" for hard situations and bad events in our lives? I struggled with this until I
realized that this passage says *in everything* not *for everything*.

The expression "in everything" is not the same as "for
everything." We don't give thanks for evil or for evil results.
But we *can* give thanks when we are in those situations because we know God is working in our lives. We can remain
grateful when our lives are touched by evil because we live in
Christ Jesus. We are living eternally and not temporally. God
gives us special attention and care because we are one of His
children. He is continually transforming us into the image of
Jesus. That's where our thanks comes in.

The well-known Bible commentator Matthew Henry made
the following entry in his diary after he had been robbed: Let
me be thankful—first, because I was never robbed before; second, because although they took my wallet they did not take
my life; third, because although they took my all, it was not
much; and fourth, because it was I who was robbed, not I who
robbed.

He was thankful in a situation created by evil.

Today's Action

♦ In everything today give thanks.

Prayer

*Father God, I pray today that Your will be done in my life. Help
me give thanks in all circumstances. Amen.*

Is It Fate?

For I was envious of the arrogant, as I saw the
prosperity of the wicked.

—Psalm 73:3

❑
❑
❑

————◇————

D avid was certainly on key with me when I look around
and see the unrighteous prospering and living to ripe
old ages, while the good people are struck down with illnesses
at a young age, children are born with defects, and floods, tor-
nadoes, and earthquakes destroy innocent people. Why?
Why? Why? Doesn't it seem unfair?

And how do we respond to these incongruities?

- ◆ We can cast away our faith and become skeptics.

- ◆ We can accept that there are dual forces at work that
  we can't do anything about; we just accept the "fate"
  of each.

- ◆ We can deny the existence of evil and accept only
  that which is good.

- ◆ We can realize that we have a sovereign God who, in
  time, will grant us understanding.

I choose the last thought knowing that in the past God has
used hardships to discipline my life. God has been loving and
just in His dealings with me. And He will be the same with
you! Life's pains and sorrows are necessary refining influences
to make us more Christlike.

Today's Action

- ◆ Trust God with your pains and sufferings.

Prayer

Father God, please help me understand when I get frustrated
with life. Let me look not to my left or to the right, but to You in times
of need. Amen.

Daily Couple Affirmation

God has good plans for us today that give us both a future and a hope.

—*Jeremiah 29:11*

God is the blessed controller of all things today.

—*1 Timothy 6:15*

We are foreordained to be molded into the image of His Son, Jesus, today.

—*Romans 8:29*

Thirsty Anyone?

Do not be overcome by evil, but overcome evil with good.

—Romans 12:21

❑
❑
❑

---◇---

Have you made anyone thirsty for God lately? As Christians we are to be the salt of the earth but too often we have turned our society over to the unrighteous to rule. We have vacated our witness in our homes, churches, schools, jobs, and communities. Our salt has lost its flavor and its preserving properties. Let me illustrate.

AIDS is a disease that destroys the immune system of the body, leaving other viruses free to attack the body. For an AIDS sufferer, a cold virus that would ordinarily cause a slight fever, drippy nose, or sore throat can turn into a life-threatening case of pneumonia. The church historically has been society's immune system. Christians have fought the diseases of our culture so that a common cold would not mean death to our society. Righteousness has kept our culture from deteriorating, but it seems that our impact is decreasing. As Christians we need to give people alternatives. We can provide options for the living, too—not just the dying. As believers our work represents the character of God. It is a testimony in the marketplace that God is alive, and He makes a difference. The world needs to hear, see, smell, taste, and feel the reality of God. Let the people see God through us!

Today's Action
- ◆ May your salt leave the shaker and touch meat.

Prayer
Father God, may I truly preserve life by using my salt effectively. Amen.

Melting Your Enemy's Heart

But I say to you, love your enemies, and pray for
those who persecute you.

—Matthew 5:44

---◇---

"L ove my enemies? Are you kidding? Why would I want to
do that? I'm so enjoying hating them." Have you ever felt
like that? I know I have. But in Matthew chapter 5, Jesus gives
three reasons to love those who persecute us:

- ◆ When we show them kindness, we are imitating our
  heavenly Father, who makes His sun rise on the evil
  and on the good, and sends rain on the just and the
  unjust (verse 45).

- ◆ We are to love our foes because there's no reward for
  loving only those who love us (verse 46).

- ◆ Gracious treatment of our enemies sets us apart
  from the ungodly. Jesus said, "If you greet your
  brothers only, what do you do more than others?"
  (verse 47).

The best way to defeat Satan in this area is to make a friend
out of an enemy. This act doesn't come naturally, and we are
only able to do it with the strength that the Holy Spirit provides.

Today's Action
- ◆ Begin to pray for an enemy who persecutes you. Let
  your prayers go before you.

Prayer
Father God, give my heart the warmth of love so that I can melt
an enemy's heart with Your love. Amen.

A Faith That Endures

Through all this Job did not sin nor did he blame God.

—Job 1:22

❏
❏
❏

————◇————

Alandholder, rancher, and community leader, Job was the most respected and influential individual in the entire region. His number-one priority was his large, active family. Despite the tremendous demands on him, he always had time for his children. They were never an interruption. And you couldn't talk to him very long without him pulling from his wallet a favorite picture of his troop; he was always eager to tell you about each of them. He knew that even though he was a very wealthy man his only legacy of significance would be his sons and daughters and grandchildren. A man living in the present but with a vision for the future, a man of God, and a man whom God had greatly blessed, Job caught Satan's eye.

In verse 8, as the Lord holds court in the heavenlies, He asks Satan, "Have you considered my servant Job? There is no one on earth like him; he is blameless and upright, a man who fears God and shuns evil."

Satan shrugs his shoulders and replies, in effect, "Sure, he's one of Your good guys. Of course, he is tight with you. He's got all the advantages. Try taking a few of his precious toys, and then see what he does. He'll surely curse You to Your face."

For reasons unknown to us, Satan is given some freedom to do what he wishes most—destroy a man's life. But the devil can't go all the way; he can only go so far. For a brief time, he is allowed to bring dark clouds over Job's life.

In a quick series of catastrophes, Job loses his business, his wealth, his health, and all ten of his children. At the height of all this his wife tells him to curse God and die (Job 2:9).

Suddenly this man of God finds himself all alone. His test was: Would he remain a real man of God, or would he reject God as soon as the good times ended and the tough times began? Is Job really a man of character or just a fair-weather follower of God?

Job remained God's man and, by doing so, offers us many valuable lessons for life. One of these lessons is that things on the outside can be taken away, but no one can ever rob us of our hearts and souls committed to the Lord or of the character that results from our commitment to Him.

We know that Job's trials strengthened his character, and people talk about the patience of Job. But he demonstrated more than patience—he shows us a faith in God that has staying power and is able to endure to the end.

Today's Action

♦ What will you do when the things of life are taken away from you?

Prayer

Father God, help me increase my faith so I can stand strong like Job. Amen.

Seeing Stress Through God's Eyes

We were burdened excessively, beyond our
strength, so that we despaired even of life.

—2 Corinthians 1:8

———◇———

Today the ever increasing pressures and stresses of living make it almost impossible to live the abundant life we all seek. Dad is pressured in down-sizing of his company, doing his job well, making the fixed payments of the household, being a loving husband and father, and leading his family as necessary. Mother has her stresses regarding proper household management, keeping the children on focus, satisfying her husband, and maintaining a proper balance in her own life.

As Christians we can endure the strain successfully if we view life's pressure situations as opportunities for us to demonstrate God's power. The following poem, which appeared in an old publication, *Record of Faith*, makes that point:

> Pressed out of measure and pressed to all length;
> Pressed so intensely, it seems beyond strength;
> Pressed in the body, and pressed in the soul;
> Pressed in the mind till the dark surges roll.
> Pressured by foes, and pressure from friends,
> Pressed into knowing no helper but God;
> Pressed into loving the staff and the rod;
> Pressed into living a life in the Lord;
> Pressed into living a Christ-life outpoured.

Today's Action

♦ Let pressure and stress teach you to live in the power of Christ.

Prayer

Father God, help me take these stressful situations and make them an opportunity for growth. Amen.

Christian Requirements

For by grace you have been saved through faith;
and that not of yourselves, it is the gift of God;
and not as a result of works, that no one should
boast.

—Ephesians 2:8,9

Several years ago a young college student asked, "How much beer can I drink and still be a Christian?" Others have asked:

- How long should I read my Bible each day?
- How long should I pray each day?
- How much money do I have to give to the church?
- Do I have to sing in the choir to be a good Christian?
- How many times a week must I be in church?
- Do I have to _____? _____? _____?

And the list goes on and on. We all want to know what the "minimum daily adult requirement" is for being a Christian. What do we really have to do, day-by-day, to get by?

Christ has freed us from bondage to minimum daily adult requirements! Our relationship with the Lord Jesus is not contingent on works; it is a gift of grace.

"So," you ask, "does that mean I don't have to do anything as a Christian? Aren't there any requirements?" The Scriptures challenge us to be like Christ, and if we are to do that we need to open the Bible and learn how Jesus lived. When we do, we see that Jesus

- studied God's Word
- spent time with believers
- prayed regularly
- served those around Him

Christ did not perform these acts because He was told to do them; He did them because He *wanted* to do them.

266

What is your minimum daily adult requirement when it comes to your spiritual health? It will be determined by love. Let your loving God guide you as you dedicate yourself to growing in the Lord.

Today's Action

♦ Ask God to help you evaluate your walk with Him. Do you need to make any changes?

Prayer

Father God, thank You for freeing me from the law and giving me grace. Amen.

God not only exists—He loves you and want you to become His child. He wants you to learn the joy of walking with Him every day, seeking His will for your life, and obeying His guidelines and moral laws.

—*Billy Graham*

The Best Prize of All

With all your acquiring, get understanding.

—Proverbs 4:7

❏
❏
❏

———◇———

A few years ago, actor Kirk Douglas wrote his auto-biography and called it *The Son of the Ragman*. In it he talks about his growing-up years with parents who had immigrated from Russia. He recalls that his mother was warm and supportive and did her best to adjust to a new country, but he remembers his father as stern, untrusting, strict, and cold. Unaccustomed to giving words of encouragement, a pat on the back, or a hug, his father remained a very distant and very private man. But then Douglas shares this story. . .

One evening at school, the young Kirk Douglas had a major role speaking, dancing, and singing in a play. He knew his mother would be there, but seriously doubted that his father would go. To his amazement and surprise, about halfway through the program, he caught view of his father standing in the back of the auditorium.

After completing the evening's program, he wanted his father to come up and congratulate him for a job well done, but true to fashion, his father wasn't able to say much. Instead, he asked his young son if he'd like to stop and get a five-cent ice-cream cone. As Kirk Douglas reflects back over all his awards in life, he prizes that five-cent ice-cream cone even more than his Oscar.

As fathers, we don't always realize the important role we play in the lives of our families. Our children hunger for our approval. They want and need to know beyond a shadow of doubt that we love them and care about what's going on in their lives. Our kids need our words, but they also need our presence. They need us to spend time with them. And sometimes giving our time says what our words can't or don't.

In today's key verse God calls us to acquire understanding, and I challenge you to work on understanding your children better. Don't assume you already know what they're thinking and feeling. Let them tell you, and then be ready to laugh when they laugh and cry when they cry. Be a dad they know really cares about the small and the big events in their lives.

Today's Action

♦ Buy each of your family members an ice-cream cone.

Prayer

Father God, help me be an encourager to my children. Amen.

Encouraging Family Partnership

He who began a good work in you will perfect it
until the day of Christ Jesus.

—Philippians 1:6

❏
❏
❏

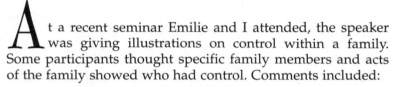

At a recent seminar Emilie and I attended, the speaker was giving illustrations on control within a family. Some participants thought specific family members and acts of the family showed who had control. Comments included:

- ◆ The breadwinner of the family has control.
- ◆ Mom does because she makes more money.
- ◆ The one who signs the checks has control.
- ◆ The one who pays the bill at the restaurant when we go out has control.
- ◆ The husband has control because he is responsible for the family.

After several more comments were written on the board, a strong male voice in the middle of the audience shouted out, "The one who controls the TV clicker has control!" Everyone laughed, knowing that he was on the right track for many families. Who would have thought this statement might really have some validity? If it is really true, then we have lost sight of God's intent for family leadership.

In Philippians 1 Paul teaches some basic principles on partnership in ministry. He wants us to see the power of God and how *He* truly is the one in control. Paul's opening words to the Philippians show us several components of encouraging your family partnership:

- ◆ thank God for all your remembrance of each family member (verse 3).

- ◆ offer prayers with joy (verse 4).
- ◆ affirm that each member is an active participant in the gospel (verse 5).
- ◆ exhibit a perspective of confidence for the future (verse 6).
- ◆ acknowledge that He who began a good work in you will perfect it (verse 6).

Such teamwork support leads to confidence. The glue that makes all this happen is the one who is really in control—almighty God. It's so refreshing to know that the possessor of the TV clicker is not ultimately in control!

Today's Action

- ◆ Recommit that God is in control of you and your family.

Prayer

Father God, I give You the control over my family. Help us become a partner with You. Amen.

What Would Jesus Do?

For you have been called for this purpose, since Christ also suffered for you, leaving you an example for you to follow in His steps.

—1 Peter 2:21

———◇———

M any years ago I read Charles M. Sheldon's book *In His Steps*, the story of a man who made a conscious effort to walk in the steps of Jesus. Before saying anything, doing anything, going anywhere, or making any decisions, he asked himself what Jesus would do and tried to do the same. Although living like Jesus was nearly impossible, this experience changed the man's life forever.

During our time on earth, daily situations will reveal our character—but will our character point others toward Jesus? We do well to look to Jesus and His example of a godly life. He showed us how to live with kindness, gentleness, sympathy, and affection. He was always loving, forgiving, merciful, and patient. He had a sense of justice and compassion for the suffering and persecuted, and He willingly took a stand for what was right in God's eyes.

Jesus also tells us that He knows our pains, our grief, and the tragedy of friends who betray us. He knows how hard it is to live in a world full of sickness and sin that we can do very little about. What we can do—and this is following in Jesus' footsteps—is bring people to Him, the one who forgives, heals, and helps. We can also let God work in our own hearts and lives so that He can make us more Christlike—and that's certainly something the world needs today.

No, we can't be exactly like Jesus. Our humanness and sin get in the way. But we can develop a teachable spirit. We can love God with all our hearts, souls, minds, and strength. We can let Him transform us into more selfless, joyful people so that our character will reveal the likeness of Jesus.

As Jesus' representatives in the world today, we walk in His steps when we help the helpless, pray for the sick, feed and clothe the homeless, and support those whom God lifts up to minister in places we can't go.

Today's Action

- ◆ Walk In Jesus' steps today. Do something that would be Christlike.

Prayer

Father God, grant me today a new revelation . . . and help me step out and trust You in a new way. Amen.

Men Need to Touch, Too

Draw near to God and He will draw near to you.
—James 4:8

———◇———

Recently a Cleveland, Ohio physician completed some research on the value and need for human beings to touch one another. He cited studies involving infants who had physical contact with their mothers soon after birth. These children smiled more, cried less, and had more interaction with their mothers than another group who didn't experience the touch technique. The first 12 hours of an infant's life are crucial—and touch, including contact by the father as well as by the mother, makes a positive impact. We have come to realize the importance of touching throughout all stages of our development and in many other situations.

In one of our marriage seminars, I shared the importance of touch. American men seem to have a more difficult time touching than woman do. Women are more likely to see a friend and go up and give her a big hug, grab an arm, or intertwine their fingers with joy. But men struggle in this area.

In essence our Scripture today is telling us, "Touch God and He will touch you." Have you ever been touched by God? Did you recognize right away that it was Him? As believers we need to stay in contact with our heavenly Father.

We reach out to God by reading Scripture daily, praying daily, interacting positively with our family and friends, being a supportive people, and recognizing daily that God is the one who directs and controls our lives.

If you don't feel that God is very close, who moved away?

Today's Action

♦ Go out and touch someone in a positive way—even if it might be uncomfortable for you.

Prayer

Father God, oh how I appreciate Your touches. Amen.

A Parent or a Friend?

I will walk within my house in the integrity of my heart.

—Psalm 101:2b

In George Washington's day, two candidates applied for a certain office. One was a warm friend and lifelong associate of Washington; the other, decidedly hostile to the politics of Washington, arrayed himself in the ranks of the opposition. It was supposed that Washington would decide for his friend; but, to the surprise of all, the other person was appointed to office.

Upon being remonstrated, Washington replied, "My friend I receive with a cordial welcome to my house and welcome to my heart; but, with all his good qualities, he is not a man of business. His opponent is, with all his hostility to me, a man of business. My private feelings have nothing to do in this case: I am not George Washington, but president of the United States. As George Washington, I would do this man any kindness in my power; but, as president, I can do nothing."

What a great example of integrity. As fathers we must step back and objectively evaluate positions. As I observe changes in our social structure I see that too many parents consider their children friends. When this happens, they lose a key parental role by making decisions based on friendship rather than good parenting.

Fathers are to be friendly and just, but, above all, they must be men of integrity.

Today's Action

♦ Are you being a parent or a friend to your children?

Prayer

Father God, help me make the tough decisions of life without compromising my status as a dad. Amen.

We find God in so many things, in flowers wakened with each Spring, in butterflies and sunsets grand, we see God's love—we touch God's hand.

To Him Be the Glory

*Oh, the depth of the riches both of the wisdom
and knowledge of God! How unsearchable are
His judgments and unfathomable His ways!*

—Romans 11:33

❏
❏
❏

In a 1973 issue of *The Pilgrim*, Dr. E. Schuyler English told of a visit to China by the Philadelphia Orchestra:

> In one city, the Chinese Philharmonic Orchestra performed Beethoven's Fifth Symphony for the visiting musicians. According to reports, it was not done very well. At the end of the first movement, the Chinese conductor passed the baton to the American conductor, Eugene Ormandy. What a transformation! As the members of the Philadelphia Orchestra listened, they were impressed in a new way with Ormandy's talent and genius. They suddenly realized that they had begun to take him for granted.

In America we live with such great abundance that we can easily forget the One who gives us so many treasures. We take God and His marvelous character and attributes for granted. We take His goodness for granted, and it becomes part of our ordinary life. In Romans 11:36, Paul says, "For from Him and through Him and to Him are all things. To Him be the glory forever."

Today's Action

◆ Think upon God's greatness; thank Him for His grace.

Prayer

Father God, I don't want to take You for granted. I recognize that all good things come from You. Thank You. Amen.

"For I know the plans that I have for you," declares the LORD, "plans for welfare and not for calamity to give you a future and a hope. Then you will call upon Me and come and pray to Me, and I will listen to you. And you will seek Me and find Me, when you search for Me with all your heart, And I will be found by you," declares the LORD....

—*Jeremiah 29:11-14*

For more information regarding speaking engagements and additional material, please send a self-addressed, stamped envelope to:

More Hours in My Day
2838 Rumsey Drive
Riverside, CA 92506

Or you can visit us on the Internet at:
www.emiliebarnes.com
or
emilie@emiliebarnes.com

Other Books by
Bob Barnes

15-Minute Devotions for Couples   15 Minutes Alone with God for Men

The 15-Minute Money Manager   What Makes a Man Feel Loved

Books by
Emilie Barnes

15-Minute Family Traditions
& Memories

15-Minute Meal Planner

15-Minute Organizer

15 Minutes Alone with God

15 Minutes of Peace with God

Beautiful Home on a Budget

Dear God

Emilie's Creative Home Organizer

Fill My Cup, Lord

Garden Pleasures Journal

If Teacups Could Talk

An Invitation to Tea

Let's Have a Tea Party!

A Little Book of Manners

More Hours in My Day

Prayers and Remembrances

Secrets of the Garden

Simply Organized

The Spirit of Loveliness

Survival for Busy Women

Taking Time for Tea Journal

Things Happen When Women Care

Time Began in a Garden

Timeless Treasures

Timeless Treasure Journal

Treasured Christmas Memories

Welcome Home

Dear Reader,

We would appreciate hearing from you regarding this Harvest House non-fiction book. It will enable us to continue to give you the best in Christian publishing.

1. What most influenced you to purchase *Minute Meditations for Men?*
   - ❑ Author
   - ❑ Subject matter
   - ❑ Backcover copy
   - ❑ Recommendations
   - ❑ Cover/Title
   - ❑ Other_____

2. Where did you purchase this book?
   - ❑ Christian bookstore
   - ❑ General bookstore
   - ❑ Department store
   - ❑ Grocery store
   - ❑ Other_____

3. Your overall rating of this book?
   ❑ Excellent   ❑ Very good   ❑ Good   ❑ Fair   ❑ Poor

4. How likely would you be to purchase other books by this author?
   ❑ Very likely ❑ Not very likely ❑ Somewhat likely ❑ Not at all

5. What types of books most interest you? (Check all that apply.)
   - ❑ Women's Books
   - ❑ Marriage Books
   - ❑ Current Issues
   - ❑ Christian Living
   - ❑ Bible Studies
   - ❑ Fiction
   - ❑ Biographies
   - ❑ Children's Books
   - ❑ Youth Books
   - ❑ Other_____

6. Please check the box next to your age group.
   ❑ Under 18 ❑ 18-24 ❑ 25-34 ❑ 35-44 ❑ 45-54 ❑ 55 and over

Mail to: Editorial Director
Harvest House Publishers
1075 Arrowsmith
Eugene, OR 97402

Name _____

Address _____

State _____ Zip _____

Thank you for helping us to help you in future publications!